THE RECOLLECTIONS
OF
WILLIAM FINAUGHTY

THE RECOLLECTIONS

OF

WILLIAM FINAUGHTY

ELEPHANT HUNTER

1864 - 1875

Peter Capstick, Series Editor

ST. MARTIN'S PRESS

NEW YORK

To the Reader:

The editors and publishers of the Peter Capstick Adventure Library faced significant responsibilities in the faithful reprinting of Africa's great hunting books of long ago. Essentially, they saw the need for each text to reflect to the letter the original work, nothing have been added or expunged, if it was to give the reader an authentic view of another age and another world.

In deciding that historical veracity and honesty were the first considerations, they realized that it meant retaining many distasteful racial and ethnic terms to be found in these old classics. The firm of St. Martin's Press, Inc., therefore wishes to make it very clear that it disassociates itself and its employees from the abhorrent racial-ethnic attitudes of the past which may be found in these books.

History is the often unpleasant record of the way things actually were, not the way they should have been. Despite the fact that we have no sympathy with the prejudices of decades past, we feel it better—and indeed, our collective responsibility—not to change the unfortunate facts that were.

—Peter Hathaway Capstick

THE RECOLLECTIONS OF WILLIAM FINAUGHTY. Copyright © 1991 by Peter Hathaway Caps All rights reserved. Printed in the United States of America. No part of this book may b used or reproduced in any manner whatsoever without written permission except in t case of brief quotations embodied in critical articles or reviews. For information, addr St. Martin's Press, 175 Fifth Avenue, New York, N.Y. 10010.

Library of Congress Cataloging-in-Publication Data

Finaughty, William.
    The recollections of William Finaughty, elephant hunter, 1864-1875
/ William Finaughty.
      p.   cm.
    ISBN 0-312-05503-X
    1. Finaughty, William. 2. Hunters—South Africa—Biography.
3. Elephant hunting—Africa, Southern.   I. Title.
SK17.F56A3   1991
799.2'6'092—dc20
[B]   90-4
                                                                              C

First Edition: January 1991
10 9 8 7 6 5 4 3 2 1

EDITOR'S NOTE TO THE REPRINT EDITION

I very much envy you if this is your first reading of William Finaughty's book, *The Re-collections of an Elephant Hunter 1864-1875*. I do not say this casually, as Finaughty's work became the single volume that started me collecting Africana. I paid six hundred dollars some ten years ago for the first edition and haven't been able to leave the peanuts alone since. What it is worth now, I couldn't say as I have never seen another "first" offered by a dealer.

"Old Bill" Finaughty is one of the original professional elephant hunters in southern Africa, part of a breed who are not misnamed as being The Company of Adventurers, as John Boyes, white King of the Kikuyu put it. Perhaps after reading this book you will agree.

The tome you hold was privately printed in the first edition by an American -- of all things -- George L. Harrison, of St. Davids, Pennsylvania, who had been hunting the Kafue River region with one of Finaughty's sons, William Jr. William told Harrison of the adventures of his father on the safari, but it wasn't until 1913 that Harrison was able to visit with the senior Finaughty, depending

EDITOR'S NOTE

upon sources, six or twelve miles from Bulawayo, The Place of Killing in Sindebele. However, the source of Harrison's private printing came not from direct ramblings by Finaughty, but rather from a series in "The Rhodesian Journal: A Weekly Newspaper of Rhodesian Information," written and edited by R. N. Hall, who had interviewed Finaughty at length. He also used Finaughty's scant notes as well as the old man's memory to write the series, which ran from June to December, 1911. There was a segment missing, but it is relatively unimportant to the action and adventure of Finaughty's life, so I have decided to leave it out of this reprinting of the first edition.

William Finaughty was born in 1843 of 1820 Settlers' stock, Britain's first attempt to inject island blood into what was then The Cape Colony of South Africa. The son of a blacksmith in Grahamstown, he had many avocations besides elephant hunting. He was a gun-runner, a storekeeper, a gambler, a trader and, dark legend has it, a counterfeiter working the race tracks of Australia. Yet, through his decade-plus of ivory hunting, he was one of the first to know Mashonaland, in what became Southern Rhodesia, then Rhodesia and, after a bloody civil war, the black one-party state of Zimbabwe. He also knew its rulers, both the despot Mzilikazi of the Matabele fugitives from Shaka Zulu, as well as the successor king, Lobengula, who was the ruler at the time of the Matabele uprisings.

EDITOR'S NOTE

By counting up his bags, we can determine that Finaughty was a great hunter as well as a fearless horseman. He killed about five hundred elephants (including being the only hunter I know of that killed more than he had bullets for) in only five years and was in a league above such as Henry Hartley, who took some 1,200 in thirty years compared to Finaughty's half a thousand in only one-sixth of the time. We know that he used muzzle loaders except for his presumably final trip to the Shashi and Semokwe rivers in 1871. They were likely four-bores, the standard elephant smooth-bore guns of Finaughty's time. On his last hunt, he used breech loaders. Of course, he hardened his pure lead with a percentage of tin or antimony which would shoot clear through a jumbo on a side angle.

Finaughty quit elephant hunting in 1871 as it was no longer practical. The big bulls would run on hearing a horse and Finaughty had a very dim view of hunting on foot. Smart man.

Certainly, "Old Bill" Finaughty was really a bit of a rogue. Only partially literate himself, he typifies the professional ivory hunter as does P. J. Pretorius, whose original manuscripts I have.

We know that he tried to take Delagoa Bay from the Portuguese with the help of the British Agent in Pretoria, but he would have none of it. We also know that Finaughty proposed to go to the

Boer government, but nobody would have any of the plot.

However, Finaughty got lucky on the winner of the Melbourne Cup in 1890, although he gambled all his winnings away. He may have been a judge of elephant flesh, but he was no soothsayer when it came to horses.

Finaughty's home life was less than idyllic. He rarely saw his wife but to father ten children, which appears to be often enough. Apparently he had quite a sense of timing....

That the children were at all literate was through the good graces of a neighbor, who tutored them in at least the first two "R's."

You might be interested to know, when you have read Finaughty's book, that the remaining cannon, ship's guns, were seen and probably are still the decorations outside the Bulawayo Museum in Zimbabwe.

Of course, I researched this foreword, especially when I found that Harrison's original private printing went to well-known African practitioners and Africana buffs. The first edition was gratis to many luminaries of this series in 1913. They included Teddy Roosevelt, his professional hunter, R. J. Cunningham, Sir Alfred Pease (*Book of the Lion*), and Denis D. Lyell. However, I had noticed scant mention by Denis Lyell. I figured that Lyell's comments would lie in *The African Elephant and Its Hunters* and I was right.

EDITOR'S NOTE

But they were not positive:

"I have tried to get Mr. Harrison's book in this country   [England] but have failed; so I suppose it was privately printed."

Aha! So Lyell did not get his copy as late as 1924. Maybe there was not enough postage....

More is Lyell's loss.

Finaughty died in 1917, at his home in Southern Rhodesia, on the farm owned by his son, William. He was seventy-four years old.

--PETER HATHAWAY CAPSTICK

PREFACE

In 1908 I had in my employ in Northwestern Rhodesia, William Finaughty, a son of William Finaughty who was one of the first white men to hunt elephants in Matabeleland. Mr. Selous says in one of his books that Finaughty stopped hunting because elephants were becoming too scarce, before he—Selous—first went to Africa. In 1913 I happened to be in Bulawayo and, having a day to spare, I visited Finaughty on a farm nearby. He gave me the numbers of the *Rhodesian Journal* containing his hunting experiences. One or two of the numbers are missing and as the journal has gone out of existence, I cannot replace them. His son had told me of his wonderful memory, and this I found confirmed by all who knew him. I found him a very slight old man with very white hair, much weakened by many attacks of fever. The value, if any, in the following pages, lies in the fact that they give a picture of a time now past which will never return.

G. L. H.

POPLAR HOUSE
   ST. DAVIDS'
      PENNSYLVANIA
May, 1916

INTRODUCTION

[JUST one word of introduction and explanation. The Editor of this paper was some months ago asked if he would undertake the task of interviewing and writing up for publication the reminiscences of the famous South African big-game hunter, "Bill" Finaughty. His reply was that he thought this renowned Nimrod had long since passed into the happy hunting grounds, but was assured that he was not only alive, but was living within a few miles of Bulawayo, and was prepared to tell of some of the things he saw and did back in those early days when Rhodesia, as it is to-day, was a part of savage South Africa, and when Mzilikatse and, after him, Lobengula, held their cruel sway. So one Sunday morning the old hunter was visited in his modest cottage, some six miles from Bulawayo, and the "recollections" were commenced. The narrative is practically in Mr. Finaughty's own words, either jotted down by him between visits or dictated to the present writer. It bears the stamp of truth, and those who know anything of the country as it was in those days— missionaries, hunters and others—will vouch for the truth of much that is here set down as to the bewildering supply of game and the prowess of the old hunters.]

CONTENTS

CHAPTER   **PAGE**

   I. MY FIRST TREK.   9

  II. BESIEGED BY LIONS—TWO MONTHS IN LAAGER   24

 III. MY SECOND TRIP—AMONG THE ELEPHANTS—
THE HARTLEY PARTY.   40

 IV. MY THIRD TRIP—TIRED OF TRADING—TURN
ELEPHANT HUNTER—NAPIER'S ALARMING
ACCIDENT—SOME BIG BAGS—5,000 LBS. OF
IVORY.   45

  V. WILD MAN OF THE WOODS—A WEIRD EN-
COUNTER—MZILIKATSE'S PEREMPTORY SUM-
MONS—A TERRIBLE TRAGEDY—DUTCH
FAMILY DECIMATED.   57

 VI. IN THE FLY COUNTRY—AN ELEPHANT ADVEN-
TURE—A LUCKY ESCAPE—THE OXEN LOST
—A SEVENTY MILE CHASE—NAPIER'S TER-
RIBLE EXPERIENCE.   65

VII. DEATH OF MZILIKATSE—IN A TIGHT CORNER—
IN THE MIDST OF HOSTILE MATABELE—AN
ANXIOUS TIME—PRESENTS FOR THE INDUNA
—REMINISCENCES OF MZILIKATSE—AN IN-
DUNA "WIPED OUT"—NAPIER'S AMUSING
ADVENTURES—END OF THE TRIP 1868.   77

VIII. WITH THE ELEPHANTS AGAIN—A TRIP WITH
CHIEF KHAMA—HUNGRY CAMP FOLLOWERS
—GIFFORD CHASED BY AN ELEPHANT—A
USELESS GUN—WE LOSE OUR BEARINGS—
A TROPICAL THUNDERSTORM—SOME NAR-
ROW RISKS.   89

IX. Lost in the Bush—My Brother's Terrifying Experience—Saved by Bushmen—A Hunter's Qualifications—Visits from Lions—A Double Fright—Pandemonium in Camp............................... 99

X. Mr. Hartley's Party Again—A Lion Adventure—The Head-man Seized—My Exploit with an Assegai—A Risky Undertaking — Cowardice of Natives — Two Plucky Picannins—Their Fight with a Lion................................... 108

XI. A Bush Thief—Bushmen's Tricky Ways—In a Hunter's Camp—Ivory, Reims and Sjamboks—Chased by a Buffalo—3,000 Pounds of Ivory—Return to Shoshong. 116

XII. Cigar and the Elephant—A Unicorn Horn—Six Elephants with Five Bullets—A Narrow Escape—The Baby Elephant and Its Mother—An Amusing Scene—A Disappointed Boer — Bushman Cattle Thief and His Deserts................. 125

XIII. Buffalo Dangers—A Savage Assault—A Wagon Accident—Among the Lions—My Horse Killed—A Day of Slaughter 134

XIV. End of the Trip—Record Elephant "Bag"—An Unconventional Smoker—A Year's Ivory: 5,000 Pounds—Adventures with the Elephants—A Cask of Peach Brandy—And How it was Tapped.............. 143

XV. Two Happy-go-lucky Hunters—How They Frightened the Elephants—Giraffe for the Pot—A Startling Experience—"Water, Water, Give us Water,"—Dan Francis' Mining Party—Quarrel With Khama's Natives...................... 152

CONTENTS

XVI. An Impudent Theft—A Headman's Haul—
More Cattle Thefts—And Swift Punishment—Adventures with Lions—An Unpleasant Corner—Between Grass Fire
and a Wounded Lion.................. 159

XVII. "Nobby" and the Elephants—Elands and
Locusts—A Cattle Raid—Playing Out
M'Tibi—How we "Lifted" His Cattle—
An Exciting Trek—A Successful Trip—
I Sell up and Settle Down—My Old
Gun's Adventures—Some Observations
on Buffalo and Tsetse Fly............. 168

XVIII. The Final Trip—A Gun-Running Expedi-
tion—Tempted by Diamonds—Cannon for
Secoconi—Arrested by Boers—A Tight
Corner—How we Tricked our Captors. 177

XIX. Tricking the Boers—How we Hid the
Cannon—and Covered Our Tracks—Arrival in Rustenburg—Before the Landdrost................................. 187

XX. Outwitting the Magistrate—My Escape
From Rustenburg—Into the Lion's Den
—An Early Morning Fright—A Dash
for the South—The Lion and the Blanket—The Funniest Fight on Earth.... 198

XXI. A Lucky Escape—Chased by a Commando
—Only a Few Hours Start—Oxen for
Horses—Another Cannon Expedition—
Arrival at Bulawayo—Purchased by
Lobengula............................. 206

XXII. An Ivory Deal—After Elephants with
Breech-Loaders—A Painful Experience—
A Cowardly Dog—A Useful Elephant
"Bag"—Adventure With a Lioness—
A Terrible Encounter—My Boy Badly
Mauled................................ 215

8 CONTENTS

XXIII. TSETSE-FLY AND BUFFALO—MY THEORY—
MY FIRST ATTACK OF FEVER—THE INJURED
NATIVE — SAD WAGON ACCIDENT — OVER-
TURNED IN A SWAMP.................... 225

XXIV. A FISHING ADVENTURE—WATCHED BY CROCO-
DILES—A FOREST TRAGEDY—LIONS, ZEBRAS
AND CROCODILES—THE SAURIANS' FEAST.. 232

XXV. FROM HUNTER TO TRADER—A BIG DEAL—
THE BASUTO WAR—IN "MAJUBA" DAYS—
ROBBED BY NATIVES—LIFE IN JOHANNES-
BURG—RETURN TO BULAWAYO—SOME FINAL
REFLECTIONS.......................... 236

THE RECOLLECTIONS
OF
WILLIAM FINAUGHTY

A Hunter's Recollections

CHAPTER I

MY FIRST TREK

BEING a harum-scarum from youth, a good horseman, and a very fair shot, I determined to get into the interior of Africa for the purpose, mostly, of shooting big game.

I left Grahamstown early in 1864, when I was 21 years of age, and came up through the Free State. The game I saw there astonished me so much that I thought it was not requisite to go much further afield. I could never have believed that such a quantity of wild animals would congregate together. As far as the eye could see it was one moving mass, tens of thousands of beautiful wild creatures of many kinds, consisting for the most part of black wildebeest, blesbok, springbok, a sprinkling of ostrich, quagga, and blue wildebeest.

I soon got tired of this kind of sport, however, for one could simply slay as much as one felt inclined to, and eventually made my way down the Vaal River, where I found Mr. E. Chapman, a local trader, on the road with his wagons to the Matabele country.

The chief of the Matabele at that time was Mzilikatse,[1] a brother of the Zulu chief, Chaka. Old Mzilikatse had made his way by force through the Transvaal, and taken possession of the country now known as Matabeleland.

Mr. Chapman had already one white man with him, a Mr. W. Francis. We were a few days at a place called Kruitfontein (powder fountain). Its water at times was undrinkable. We made a start to the Vaal River, which was very full, but we got all the goods over in a boat, and then we tied large logs of dry willow-wood and a couple of casks under the wagons and floated them in that way over the river, the boat in front towing them. It was hard work, and took us just four days. We at once started for Kuruman, a very pretty place. The Rev. Robert Moffat was there, also Mr. John Chapman. We stopped at Kuruman about a fortnight, and then started on a long, dreary journey, skirting the Kalahari desert and passing through the Bechuana villages—Ian Missiby, Kanye, Molepolole and Shechillies. Before us was a stretch of 140 miles, with very doubtful water, but we were very lucky and got water about 20 miles from Shechillies. The roads were very heavy with sand and quite 18 inches deep. We were very lucky

---

[1] Mosilekatse.

again in getting a little muddy water at a place called Beatlanamie, although the buffalo had been having a drink during the night and made the water a bit muddy.

After having something to eat, Chapman proposed to try and get a shot at the buffalo. The horses were saddled, and Chapman and boy[1] and myself followed the spoor a short distance and saw them. The bush being pretty thick we got parted, unluckily, and I managed to shoot a very fat cow.

Chapman nearly got caught by an old bull which he did not see until he had got nearly past him. The buffalo made a rush at Chapman, who started to get away, but, the bush being very thick and a fallen tree across his path, he was checked. He looked back and saw the buffalo close behind him and death staring him in the face. On the spur of the moment he threw his gun at the beast. The weapon caught him on the back, and this distracted his attention from Chapman for a few seconds and gave him a chance of getting away. I went afterwards with Chapman to get his gun.

We stopped the day over to cut up the meat of the cow I had shot. It was good eating, for buffalo is really first-class beef. We started again, and hearing that the Pan[2] Selinya, about 20 miles

---

[1] Native servant of any age.
[2] Pool of water.

ahead, had plenty of water, we got there all right, only to be confronted with another stretch of over 40 miles, with no water and very heavy road. We arrived at Shoshong, a very large Bechuana village of about 80,000 inhabitants, with Seccommie as chief. There were also two missionaries, the Rev. John McKenzie and Rev. Rodger Price. It was one of the principal trading stations in the interior on account of three roads meeting—one from Lake N'gama, one from Zambezi, and the other from the Matabele country. We stayed quite a fortnight here, and the day we trekked away I was quite delighted, for it was absolutely the most filthy place I ever saw. We trekked to the first water, Magalappe, about 20 miles.

Next day Mr. Price and the young chief, with a lot of followers, came to us and said they were going to shoot some game for meat. We went out together, about six of us, and that day I saw the most glorious sight I ever witnessed. We had scattered out, Mr. Price being on my right, when he came racing along by the side of about 300 to 400 giraffe. It was a wonderful and beautiful sight. It seemed a pity to shoot them, but we bottled up sentiment and got five of them. The meat was put on the wagons, also the skins. Nothing was wasted. That night I had a grilled steak of giraffe, which I thought delicious, and I still think giraffe meat the best of all. With such a store of meat as this there was no fear of starving now.

We left the young chief Khama and Mr. Price, and travelled only in the day time, on account of lions. After about six days' travelling we came to a place called Serowe, where one could get water by digging the dirt out, and this we had to do. I asked Chapman if he was going on that morning and he replied: " Yes, as soon as the oxen have had a feed." I said I would go on along the road, because as a rule I used to walk ahead of the wagons. I started and thought I would get to the next water, Gookure, about 18 miles ahead. It was a good hard tramp but I got there all right, saw a koodoo near the water and shot it, made a fire and had a feed, and cut off a leg of the buck and hung it up in a tree. I waited but there was no sign of the wagons, and as the day was drawing in I thought I had better go back and pick the wagons up. I walked till my legs ached, but still no wagon, and I wondered what could have happened. At last about midnight, utterly worn out, having walked 36 miles, I arrived at the spot where I started from, and the wagons were still there! They had never started; thought they would wait another day! After that experience I took precious good care never to go on ahead until I had seen the wagons on the move.

Just after I had got to sleep I was aroused by the roar of a lion close to camp. I don't know whether he had been stalking me and was annoyed at losing his supper. Anyway, Chapman called out and asked me if I had heard it and suggested that we go out and get a shot at him.

I said I was ready, but I noticed that he did not go too far from the wagons. At any rate we waited till the lion roared again, and I let drive at the spot where the sound came from. The old lion immediately let out a roar of rage, and started to growl and kick up a most unearthly din. After a time he took himself off, and that was the last we heard of him.

The next morning I saw the wagons moving before I ventured to step on ahead.

About four miles along the road I noticed a vast number of vultures sitting in the mopani trees. I sauntered over to see what might be the cause of this congregation, and as I approached the vultures flew away. To my amazement, I suddenly came face to face with a lioness! I was considerably startled, but I at once raised my old muzzle-loader, which was always kept loaded, and killed her with one shot. After re-loading I walked over to where she lay, and found close to her the remnants of a wildebeeste recently killed, but all the flesh had been cleaned off and nothing but the bones remained. I thought to myself that the lioness had been doing herself pretty well, but I was too hungry to take much notice of it, and promptly made up my mind to kindle a fire with a view to enjoying a few grilled marrow-bones. Then I got another shock, for as I was picking up a few sticks for this purpose an old male lion calmly stood up right in front of me! He had obviously been within a few yards of me for some minutes, but was too gorged with meat to trouble himself to move till I was almost on top of him.

To say that I dropped the sticks like hot coals, jumped for my gun and pulled the trigger is but faintly to express the celerity of my movements. I hit him fairly, but he bounded away, and I did not follow. I was too hungry.

I lit the fire, and was in the middle of an interesting culinary operation when Chapman came up, and, seeing me roasting the big marrow bones over the flames, burst into a peal of laughter at the idea of a man eating of an animal in the bush when the cause of its death was unknown to him.

In reply, I merely directed his attention to the body of the dead lioness, which he had not previously seen, and also pointed to the blood spoor of the old lion, using my hot marrow-bone as a pointer. Chapman quickly stopped laughing at my apparent " greenness," and on following up the blood spoor found the old male lion *in extremis,* my bullet having gone through his lungs.

Chapman and I then walked along the road together, waited at midday for the wagons, and had the usual midday meal—a cup of tea and a sardine—and then I went on ahead alone. When I came to the tree where I had previously killed the koodoo and had hung up a leg for the previous evening's meal, I found, as might have been expected, that the vultures had cleared everything but the bones. That night at the water I got a shot at a rhinoceros, but he managed to get away, leaving a blood spoor. We followed it a little way next morning, but as it took us off our route we decided not to follow it up, and pushed on to Macloutsie River, where the usual practice of scraping out the sand to get water for the oxen had to be followed. In due course I will tell of an extraordinary sight I saw at this spot on my return journey.

From this stage we pushed ahead rapidly. Chapman was very keen upon getting along, and though the spoor of all sorts of game, including elephants, was abundant, we did not trouble to go after them. Next day we got to the Tati where

Chapman and I, in the course of a stroll, fired simultaneously at an old giraffe bull that we had stalked to within 200 yards. The two bullets together killed him on the spot. He was a lovely animal, fat as butter, the fattest giraffe I have ever seen. With a pleasant recollection of our previous feed of delicate giraffe meat we went forward to cut him up, but to our disgust he smelt so rank that his flesh was absolutely uneatable. Robbed in this inglorious manner of an evening meal, we returned to camp and next morning we took Francis to have a look at him. We were treated to an amazing spectacle. There were at least ten to a dozen lions round the carcase, some tearing away at the flesh, others lying down, full to repletion. We watched them for a few seconds and it really was a picture worth looking at. Then Francis fired at one of them, more to frighten them than anything else. I don't know whether he struck the one he aimed at; anyhow they all cleared off.

It took us five days from Tati to reach the entrance to the Matabele country. Here we were stopped by the Matabele guards and our arrival reported from there by messenger. As Chapman had been in before we were not detained at the entrance, as strangers always were until the chief's permission had been received. We were allowed to proceed very slowly, but by the end of July we had arrived at Mzilikatse's kraal, which was then on the Bembesi.

He seemed very pleased indeed to see us but he was particularly keen upon knowing whether Francis and I were " English " and put the question several times. He had a great dislike of Dutchmen and seemed a little suspicious about us, at first. However, we were able thoroughly to satisfy him as to our English antecedents and then all was well.

The old chief was a physical wreck. His lower limbs were paralysed and whenever he moved he was carried in an armchair by four strapping wives. He was not a very big man—about 5 ft. 8 in., I should say, but very square-shouldered. He was a good-tempered old chap, in spite of occasional outbursts of violence against his people, and we were continuously having conversation with him, when he would laugh and joke with us in the most genial manner.

It was on the occasion of this visit that I had my first and probably my finest view of the Matabele army in its prime. It was the time of their New Year and a big dance was on, night and day. The warriors, who numbered about 25,000, were all in their war-dress, wearing their plumes and carrying assegais and shields, and they made a wonderful and impressive spectacle. To see thousands of them dancing round the camp fires at night, to listen to their singing and the dull noise of the drums, and to hear the thud of their bare feet on the earth was to get an impression of the might of the Matabele that to a youngster like myself was thrilling in the extreme. It might to some people seem to be dangerous for three white men to be in the midst of this huge army, worked up into a frenzy with the dancing, the beer and the general excitement; but, of course, we were as safe as we would be in Bulawayo to-day. Not one of us gave it the least thought. Once the chief had given us permission to enter the country there was no danger and we walked among the braves with complete confidence.

Just for curiosity Francis and I went round the kraal after the oxen had been slaughtered for the feast and counted 540 beasts lying dead—a very respectable butcher's bill.

Horse sickness was as deadly in those days as now; in fact much more so. Of the 17 horses we brought up with us, 14 died within 30 hours of each other. It was a heavy loss and caused us some amount of inconvenience.

We remained for several months at the royal kraal. We did not occupy any of the huts but took our wagons inside the kraal and slept in them, as we had done throughout the journey. It was a fairly lazy and interesting time for me. Chapman spent his time trading, and managed to secure about 5,000 lbs. of ivory, also a few oxen, sheep and goats. I, having nothing better to do, roamed about shooting small game all of which came in very useful for the pot, while the natives also keenly appreciated the many buck I was able to shoot for them. Frequently a commando of young Matabeles would come out with me for a day's shooting and we used to have some exciting times together. On several occasions I got more meat than they could carry home.

One day some women came in with an exciting story that a herd of elephants had arrived in the mealie lands, had taken complete possession and would not let the women gather in the corn. Mzilikatse at once sent for Chapman and asked him to go and shoot them. Chapman and I mounted our horses, put a boy on the third and after a long ride we came to the lands and there, true enough, were the elephants, who showed no disposition to move. We each got in a shot and killed an elephant apiece. The others immediately cleared into the adjoining bush. Leaving the boy behind we retraced our steps to the wagons, but it was midnight before we arrived and both we as well as the horses were nearly worn out with fatigue.

We hear a good deal now-a-days of the problem of the sexes and people often say that in the " old days " the natives were much more moral than they are to-day. That may be so, but in those days they had a way of dealing with offenders that was not calculated to encourage others to go and do likewise. I was taking a stroll one evening looking for a chance buck, when underneath a large tree I saw a native with his head battered in. I was a bit startled, and wondered what grim tragedy had been enacted.

I happened to glance up into the tree and there, well above my head, were two native women hanging by their necks! I had heard hints of Mzilikatse's methods of dispensing justice and upon making discreet enquiries ascertained the drama of which these three dead bodies were the sequel. It appeared that the women were two of the King's numerous wives. They lived together in one hut, this being the custom so that they could be not only company but a check upon each other's doings. However, in this case the check was ineffective. A native brave had become enamoured of one of the wives and used to visit her at night, the other woman, if she knew, taking no notice.

The amour was discovered at last and Mzilikatse decreed the usual punishment—the woman to be hanged and the man to have his skull smashed with a knobkerrie. The second woman was ordered to be hanged by the side of the guilty wife because she had not reported to Mzilikatse the other's marital misdemeanour! In this crude way the Chief kept his wives up to the mark and struck fear into the hearts of his people. While on this subject I may here state that the Matabele women bore a splendid reputation for virtue so far as the white visitors to the country were concerned. Whether they were so among themselves I cannot say, but the punishment above mentioned would appear sufficient to keep them in the straight and narrow path.

Another instance of Mzilikatse's barbarity occurred during our stay. An impi about 2,000 strong had gone out on one of their periodical raids, the weak Mashonas being their objective, as usual. They took sufficient oxen to kill on the outward journey, relying upon their successful foray to give them more than sufficient meat for the return. For once, however, they got the worst of the encounter. The Mashonas put up a great fight and beat the Matabeles off.

They returned empty-handed, and very sick and sorry, after having been away for about a month. Mzilikatse's wrath was appalling. He expressed his disgust in no measured terms and then without giving them any food set them dancing. And he kept them at it for four days and nights without cessation! The only food they had was the little they could pick up from the others who threw scraps of food towards them. It was terrible to see these leg-weary, heart-broken, starving men dancing hour after hour till their eyes drew back into their sockets and delirium crept into their brains. Still they danced on, while the Old Man sat before them and they knew only too well that to stop when he had told them to go on would be to stop forever. It was the most hideous dance of death I ever saw or heard of. It was "Dance or die."

Francis and I were present when Mzilikatse announced his intention of giving them some food. A few of them were brought in and sat round in a half-moon in front of the chief. Some raw meat was brought in on something like a butcher's tray and the induna told them to eat. One man seized a leg of mutton and bit a huge piece out of it. He was so ravenous that he could not wait to masticate it, but took another mouthful, trying to dispose of the first piece by swallowing it. The lump of raw flesh stuck in his throat and the poor wretch commenced to cough and choke.

"Take the dog away!" said Mzilikatse. They dragged him out of the half-moon, gave him one swinging blow by the side of the ear with a knobkerrie, and he dropped dead.

CHAPTER II

I HAVE mentioned what a splendid sight the Matabele army presented in its prime. The great herds of cattle were no less inferior in interest. There were enormous numbers, for cattle represented the Matabele idea of wealth, and as Mzilikatse had very strict ideas with regard to the royal prerogative they were not killed off at an excessive rate. As Matabeleland was and is still one of the finest cattle-raising countries in the world, small wonder that the herds originally brought in from Zululand had multiplied in an unprecedented manner.

The cattle had been distributed between the various kraals, in charge of the respective indunas, and it was a picture to see them going out each morning in charge of the herds, or returning at nightfall to the kraals. Although there would be two or three colours in each kraal yet when they went out to graze each colour would be kept separate, and as the cattle had been separated in this way from the time they were calves, they sorted themselves out almost of their own accord. To see a great herd of blacks or of reds marching off to the grazing grounds was to witness a picture that we do not see in these days.

Speaking of oxen reminds me of an extraordinary sight I saw, and illustrates the vast number of Matabele there were in those days and their unwavering obedience to the Chief. There was a " wild " ox reported to Mzilikatse, an animal that had taken it into its head to break loose from its quiet traditions, and would no longer take its usual place with the kraal cattle. The Chief told his people to bring it in. They immediately proceeded to teach the ox the lesson of his life. I don't know how many hundred men went after it, but I saw them return—a solid mass of men packed closely together, with the ox in the centre high in the air standing on their shoulders!

It was the noise of their singing that attracted my attention to the incident. They came marching in, some two or three hundred strong, chanting in exultant terms of how they had captured the culprit who had dared to break away from the care of the great Chief. The terrified animal, bellowing and trembling with mingled fear and rage, was carried high above them till it was set down, amid jubilant shouts, at the kraal, where it received such a lesson admonitory and otherwise as to cure it of any further tendencies to roam.

This incident reminds me of another curious story, which was told to me at the time, and I was assured that it had actually occurred. Crocodiles, it appeared, were under the special protection of Mzilikatse, who would not allow any of them to be killed. They occasionally took toll of cattle, also sheep, goats and even a human being, but this was regarded as the proper order of things. I could not ascertain whether there was anything in the nature of worship of these animals, but I subsequently learned that it was as much as a man's life was worth to shoot one.

One day it was reported to the Chief that a child had been taken at the river by a hungry crocodile and the distressed people wished to know what the Chief would have them do.

" Bring them both to me," was the laconic reply.

Now, it is well known that the crocodile never eats its victims immediately they are captured. The usual plan is to pull the prey under the water and drown it and then carry it to some hole, possibly under the projecting root of a tree, where the body remains in this " larder " until it is " high " and tender enough for the crocodile's epicurean tastes. The natives evidently knew this well enough.

How they did it I don't know, but I was assured that upon receiving the Chief's instructions a huge crowd of them marched to the scene of the tragedy, and though the river was swarming with crocodiles the braves plunged into the water, captured the crocodile that was alleged to be the culprit—he was an enormous fellow—and recovered the child's body.

With the dead child and the live crocodile held high above them, they returned to the kraal, where the Chief administered justice.

I have always regretted that I was not sufficiently curious to ascertain what actually happened. I do not think he would have ordered it to be killed. Probably it would be severely reprimanded and returned to its lair. Possibly some ceremony connected with " medicine " would take place. I was too young to interest myself in the matter, being chiefly concerned with the almost incredible feat of capturing such a huge creature alive and carrying it on their shoulders to the presence of the Chief. One can imagine the sort of song they would sing to a crocodile in such circumstances and how the power, might, majesty and dominion of the great Mzilikatse would be impressed upon the struggling saurian.

During the whole time I was in the country I never saw a sign of gold among the Matabele. If they knew of the value, or the presence in the country, of the precious metal they made no attempt to exploit it. Personally I do not think they had the slightest idea of its use or value or even of its whereabouts. Their idea of wealth was cattle, ivory, guns, ammunition, beads, etc.

I might say here that Mzilikatse would not permit any prospecting in the country. He knew just enough to know that there was in the ground that which, if discovered, would cause an influx of white men. He did not mind a few traders or hunters, for they brought him things from civilization which were desirable, but beyond that he did not mean to go, and to ensure this the artful old man put a guide at every white man's disposal from the moment he entered the country till the time he left. He was a guide it was true, but he was also a spy, and one's every action was faithfully reported to the Chief. And knowing what Mzilikatse was, very few ventured to defy his explicit instructions with regard to looking for forbidden things. I never heard any other white men make reference to the presence of either gold or diamonds in the country save one— Baines, the explorer. We met him at the Mangwe and he mentioned that he had found small gold nuggets on the river Umyati, which would be somewhere about Que Que, but we took little notice of it. The men who ventured into Matabeleland in those days were not gold hunters and did not trouble their heads about the matter. Ivory and cattle were their main consideration.

The old Chief treated us excellently, right throughout our stay. He sent us beer and meat almost every day, and showed his friendly interest in us in unmistakable fashion. He could not get it out of his head, however, that Francis and I by some possibility might be Boers, despite our denials, and he would frequently bring the conversation round to that point, and ingenuously ask us if after all we were sure we were not Boers? I don't know what would have happened if we had said that we were, but I fancy that the very least would have been an immediate ejection from the territory, if nothing worse.

I cannot refrain at this stage from telling a story that was told us by Mr. Thomas, father of the present Native Commissioner. He had arrived from the South, and told us that on his way he passed the Rev. Sykes, who, with his wife, had been camped for about a fortnight on the northern bank of the Shoshong. An impudent small dog was of the missionary's party—a perky, plucky little beast that would bark at anything living.

Well, one night the missionary and his wife were asleep inside their beautiful bucksail wagon, when the small dog commenced barking in its usual furious way. They took little notice, for its yapping was a frequent occurrence.

Then they heard noises as if a couple of dogs were jumping around each other with, however, only the small dog barking. The jumping about lasted a few seconds, and then there was a loud noise as some big body came crashing up against the tightly fastened sail.

The reverend gentleman instantly sprang out of bed, groped round for his spectacles, struck a match, opened the flap—and looked straight into the eyes of a big lion which, having failed to catch the dog, was evidently wondering whether the occupants of the wagon would make good eating.

It seems unnecessary to add that the reverend gentleman withdrew his head without wasting any time. He groped for his gun, which, although loaded, was uncapped, and then followed an anxious interval while the devoted pair struck the exasperatingly slow old " tandstiker " lucifer matches and frantically searched for the caps. The reverend gentleman was short-sighted and could not see too well, while the nerves of neither could be said to be particularly steady, with old man Leo outside the flap breathing hard and sniffing in a horribly suggestive manner.

However, after what seemed an age, the caps

were found, and a shot through the bucksail scared the lion away, the small dog celebrating the retreat of its enemy with a perfect volley of insulting barks.

I have omitted to mention that shortly after our arrival at Mzilikatse's kraal an old induna arrived and reported the presence of some wagons and three white men at Mangwe Pass. He said they had several Zulu boys with them from Natal. Mzilikatse immediately forbade them to enter the country, and ordered them to return from whence they came. I shall have more to say of this party later on.

About the first week in October we started on our return journey. We travelled very slowly on account of the sheep and goats—about 500—that Chapman had traded from the Matabele. We got among elephants close to the Ramaquabane, but made a poor business of it. I knew absolutely nothing about shooting elephant, and Chapman knew very little more. If we had had more experience we might have got a fine haul. As it was, we only managed to get one apiece, and the ivory in these was not up to much.

And now I come to the incident of the wagons above referred to, which had been turned back from the Matabele country several months previously.

The morning we left Shashi, Chapman, myself

and the boy mounted the horses for the purpose of stalking a fat giraffe, and so replenishing the larder. Our luck was out; we saw plenty of other game, but no sign of giraffe, and as it was giraffe we were after we did not fire.

During the afternoon we made our way down to the Macloutsie Drift. We noticed as we approached a large dark patch that roused our curiosity. It was certainly not there when we crossed on the upward journey, and we could not imagine what it might be. At first we thought it must be a herd of elephants, but it did not move as we approached, and we were left in doubt as to what it was until we were quite close, when we saw that it was a laager formed of a very high and thick fence of thorn bush, enclosing two wagons.

The meaning of such a defensive structure was quite beyond us until we arrived close to the fence, when three white men welcomed us in terms of most heartfelt gratitude, like men who had just been relieved from a long and terrible siege.

They had a pitiful tale to tell. They said they were the people who had been turned back by Mzilikatze as mentioned above and that they had been camped here ever since, *besieged by lions!*

Chapman, inclined to look upon this statement as a trifle overdrawn, was about to turn his horse loose when they implored him not to let the horses out of control as they were surrounded by lions!

At this juncture a Zulu boy climbed out of the front of the wagon and shouted: " There is one lying under the tree over there! " We turned and looked, and sure enough there was some object that Chapman pronounced to be a lion.

We immediately saddled up again and rode to the spot, which was not more than a hundred yards away, and as we neared the tree a lion sprang up and cleared into the scrub.

Chapman called out to me to keep down the river. This I at once did, and as I was galloping through some thick, low scrub I saw the lion. Heading my horse to turn it out into more open country I managed to get my quarry out of the bush and at the first shot brought him down.

Almost immediately I heard Chapman fire and then followed a tremendous roaring. Galloping towards the sound I was just in time to see him get in a second shot which finished his lion off. Upon examining the carcase we found that the first shot had only hit him in the foot, hence the terrible roaring I had heard.

We rode back to the laagered wagons and asked the three gentlemen to come out and have a look at the dead lions, but this they absolutely and emphatically refused to do, saying they had seen enough live ones to last them for the rest of their natural lives!

When we had off-saddled and tethered the horses we went inside the laager and they told us one of the strangest stories I have ever heard.

The party, which included Mr. Throgmorton, Mr. de Barry and Mr. Page had, it appeared, fitted out an elaborate outfit in Natal for the purpose of hunting in the interior of Africa. They had two fine wagons, spans of oxen, several horses, a most complete and elaborate equipment and, worst of all from their point of view, several Zulu servants. Probably they thought that their affinity to the Matabele would render their presence of great assistance in obtaining admission to, and progress through, the Matabele country. On the contrary they realised when too late that the Zulus were *anathema* to Mzilikatse, who had no cause to love, or to regard with anything but suspicion, the presence of members of the race from which he and his people had cut themselves adrift. Anyway the presence of these Zulu servants had caused Mzilikatse to turn the whole party back. As things were, however, it was probably the best thing that could have happened to them, for a more helpless lot of men on the veld I never saw. If they had once got

adrift in the wild Matabele or Mashona country
among the big game I am perfectly certain that
some if not all of them would assuredly have been
either killed or lost.

After they were turned back they camped by
the Macloutsie River. The first thing that happened to them was the lions stampeding their oxen.
After tremendous difficulty they succeeded in recovering five of them, but shortly after they got
them back to the wagons they lost them again, this
time for good. By this time they had only one
horse left, and this, too, was killed by lions. They
thought they would have some revenge and so fixed
up a gun near the carcase with a line to the trigger,
and during the night, when the lions came for their
supper, the gun was discharged and one of the
animals was killed though the party did not know
this till some days later.

They were now placed in a most unenviable
and dangerous position. With their oxen and
horses gone they were unable to move the wagons
and none of them would face the risks of going on
foot to secure assistance. Meantime the lions, that
had done so well out of the party, hovered around
them, with ominous persistency. Every day they
could be seen prowling round the camp, while at

night their roaring caused the most acute apprehension in the minds of the luckless hunters.

Though only a short distance from the river, the task of securing water for drinking purposes was one of extreme danger. Lions were frequently seen by the boys when they went to get water, and on one occasion the boy was " treed " by the brutes and had to remain in the branches for some three hours before the hungry animals turned their attention to more promising quarry and allowed him to get away.

So the time drearily passed. No help appeared on the scene; their stock of provisions was limited and they were at their wits' ends. Terrified by the encircling lions they had put the boys to work to cut down a huge quantity of thorn bush, and with this they completely encircled the wagons with a thick hedge some six to eight feet high. Only one small opening was left, through which a boy crept once a day to get water, and this was immediately closed behind him. To make their pitiable plight worse, all their boys, save one, deserted, and they saw nothing before them but to sit down and wait till relief in some shape or form, or starvation, solved the problem for them. They had been inside their zareba for *two months* and to such an extent had the lions got upon their nerves that the white men

positively refused to go outside on any excuse whatsoever, and there they had remained cooped up in
this pitiable, terrified state all this time.

What would have happened to them if we had
not turned up when we did is hard to say. Their
provisions were practically finished, their nerves
were quite unstrung, and all initiative had left them.
Their relief at our arrival was unbounded.
Whether they would have made some determined
move to get out of their troubles if we had not
turned up I do not know. Anyway, we were looked
upon as saviours. Chapman managed to rake up a
span of oxen for them; their two wagons were tied
together so that the one span could pull both, and
in this manner we got them back out of the
wilderness.

Our journey back to Shoshong was necessarily
slow, and it was, at the same time, uneventful. The
only incidents I remember were my success in shooting a couple of ostriches, also a lot of small game
for the pot.

While at Shoshong the lions got among the missionaries' cattle and killed four of them. We white
men, accompanied by about 400 natives, thereupon
organised a big lion hunt. We had a great day's
sport, rounded the lions up, and I was lucky enough
to get first shot, my bullet hitting a big lion fairly

in the ribs and bringing him down. There were only two of the beasts, but the other one managed to slip away unhurt.

We stayed at Shoshong until the end of November, and a month later we arrived at Kuruman. I remained there looking after Mr. John Chapman's store while he went to the Colony to replenish his stocks of goods. It was a lonely four months for me, and I was only too glad when my vigil was over. Some people speak of the loneliness of the veld. It was never lonely to me, and certainly not so lonely as looking after an up-country store in those days.

Thus ends my first trip into the interior. Even to-day I look back upon it with something like admiration, for it must not be forgotten that I was only a youngster of 21 years of age, and with no previous experience of the sort of life it would mean. One had to rely all the time upon one's own resources, for we could not afford to carry huge stocks of provisions on what was essentially a trading trip. Many and many a time I have gone hungry and been nearly starved, for one could not always get a buck, and if one failed in this respect we just had to go hungry till the Fates were kind again. The daily ration was a biscuit and a cup of coffee in the morning, a cup of tea, a biscuit and one tin of sardines

among the three of us at midday, and at night coffee
and a biscuit again. We hadn't room in the wagons
to carry anything more elaborate for such a long
trek, and even then, living on this most meagre fare,
our stock of provisions for such a long trip was by
no means a small consideration. I can truthfully
say that hunger sharpened my hunter's wits. Many
a weary tramp I have performed in order to " fill
the pot." In some parts, of course, the game was
so thick you could kill it " from the wagon," so to
speak. In another place we would not see an animal
for days together, and these were the times when
we learned that a tin of sardines among three
hungry men was not exactly a Grand Hotel
banquet.

CHAPTER III

My second trip in 1865 was rather tame. This time I went in " on my own " as a trader. I left Kuruman in March, and worked my way to Shoshong. Here I remained trading till November, when, upon the arrival of Mr. E. Chapman from the Matabele country, I replenished my stock from his remnants and left for Mzilikatse's territory. I had no adventures worth noting on the way in. When I got there I traded a little ivory and about 200 oxen, and then turned again to the South. Here I fell in with Mr. Hartley's shooting party. It was a big crowd of white men. There was old Mr. Hartley, his three sons, Fred, Tom and " little Willie "—who I may mention here subsequently died up-country, and after whom the Hartley Hills are affectionately named — also his stepson, Maloney; Mr. S. Liesk, of Klerksdorp; " Big " Phillips, Mr. Gifford, and a captain of some militia corps whose name has slipped my memory, and a Dutchman.

I had no horse, so Mr. Hartley lent me one to shoot with, I to give him half of all I shot. The

40

horse turned out to be a brute and completely spoiled. None of the party could do anything with him, and that was why he had been lent to me! I was reckoned a good horseman, but he managed to unseat me the first time I got into the saddle. The girth broke and I came a purler, saddle and all. He scored there, but I soon taught him better manners, and after a very short time he grew so quiet and tame that he would allow me to shoot from his back. This horse, I may mention, was in excellent condition on account of not having done any work, while all the others were extremely poor from being severely worked, while at the same time they had had very little food, the party being unable to obtain grain for them in the Mashona country.

Our first trip from the wagons was for elephant. We left the wagons, all mounted, in the early morning, and in the afternoon we came across four bull elephants. They bolted, and we set off in hot pursuit. I was the first to come up with them owing to the fact that my horse was in better condition than theirs. As a result I bagged all four of the elephants, and I certainly regarded that as a very fair day's achievement on a horse that nobody else would ride.

That same week I got three more bulls out of a very large herd, while the whole of the Hartley party only got two between them. I did not like their style of hunting a little bit. They never secured a large bag. Instead of each man selecting his own animal, they all bunched together and shot at the same elephant until he was down, and then, if opportunity permitted, went after another. Of course, they got very little in this way. I suppose the chief reason for this, at any rate so far as the boys were concerned, was the necessity for them to keep together to look after the old gentleman, who was very shaky on his feet. If he had allowed them to go off each on his own line they would have done far better, but they had to do as he told them, and so I did as much, or more, myself as they did all told. The old man was certainly a drawback in this respect.

The next time we came up to elephants we all made a terrible bungle of the business. I shot a cow and when she fell I saw she had a small calf with her. The little thing refused to leave its mother and to follow the herd. It remained by its fallen mother's side till I came up, when it immediately ran towards me in the most plaintive way. My horse was frightened and got out of its way, not understanding or appreciating the little creature. I just looked to see that the cow was dead and then turned to go back to the wagons. The baby elephant, acting upon some instinct that made it regard me as its protector—after I had slain its mother—persistently followed me all the way back to the wagons. When I got there with my strange follower I found, to my amazement, that a similar experience had befallen the Hartleys and a baby elephant, a little larger than mine, had followed them back to the wagons, mutely claiming their protection. For a moment we scarcely appreciated the position of foster-mothers to two unwieldy babies of this description but then we thought of the high prices young elephants fetched at the coast and we realised that if we could keep them alive and take them with us we should do even better with them than we should from the ivory of the dams we had shot.

Unfortunately they did not live long, although we had two cows with us giving milk. We gave them plenty of milk, also some gruel, but the food did not suit them. Dysentery set in and they died about three weeks later.

After this I had to give my horse up. I had shot seven bull elephants and one cow and I could see that while the old gentleman appreciated his half of the ivory he did not like to see my eight tusks leaving him. Human nature, I suppose! I was offered another horse but I declined, and left the party.

I hurried on with all possible speed to Shoshong, where I fell in with a hunter from the Zambesi, one Martinus Swaarts. I sold him 50 oxen, for which I got paid in ivory, and then pushed on without delay to Kuruman, at which place I arrived after an absence of exactly 12 months. I certainly had no reason to complain of the result of my first venture, for both in cattle and ivory the trip had proved most successful, for a youngster.

Mr. John Chapman was away when I arrived but he returned from a trip to the Colony a few days later and I very quickly disposed of the results of my trip and made arrangements to return.

CHAPTER IV

MY THIRD TRIP—TIRED OF TRADING—TURN ELEPHANT
HUNTER—NAPIER'S ALARMING ACCIDENT—SOME BIG
BAGS—5,000 LBS. OF IVORY

My third trip was distinctly for trading purposes and was entered upon in April, 1866. With
the proceeds of the previous venture I was able to
carry a fairly heavy stock and looked forward to a
highly profitable expedition.

My journey to Shoshong was without incident
but extremely lonesome and I was glad when at
the end of May I arrived at my destination. I at
once set to work and built myself a large hut to
trade in and sent a letter to Mr. John Chapman
asking him to come up or send some one up for
my produce. Towards the end of the year he
arrived himself bringing with him a big load of
goods, all of which I bought from him.

Once more I made a start for the Matabele
country, but by the time I had traded all my goods
for ivory and oxen I began to fancy that hunting,
not trading, was my specialty especially in view of
the success I had achieved during my previous short
spells among the elephants. So when a few months

45

later (early in 1867) the Hartley party came in again I decided to join them.

Leaving my wagon and the oxen at the missionaries', I took only two horses and two boys, not intending to stay with the party for very long. My main object was to see something of the elephant country, of which I then knew very little. Once more my luck was in for I soon had nine elephants to my credit. It was clear that the party did not like it, and as it soon became too uncomfortable to remain, I left the ivory with them, with a request that they would bring it out on their return, and I pushed ahead entirely alone save, of course, for my two boys and the horses.

On the road, I shot eight elephants, all cows, but carrying fair tusks. Luckily, I came across a Cape Colony boy [1] coming out from the Zambesi, and I induced him to allow his boys to carry my ivory as far as Inyati.

My success with the gun having definitely decided me to follow a hunter's rather than a trader's calling, I started at once for Shoshong to thoroughly equip myself for the new life. Good horses were absolutely essential for this purpose, and I found it essential to go as far as Shechillies. There I had to give £60 apiece for two, but as they were guaranteed against horse sickness, the price could not

---

[1] Cape Colony boy or Cape boy—a native of Cape Colony of mixed blood.

be regarded as excessive, especially in those days. It may be of interest to mention here that one of them was the finest shooting horse I ever crossed, and after using him for three seasons, I sold him for £300 worth of ivory. It may sound like a fairy story, but it is sober fact, and he was worth it. He was a powerful bay standing about 14 hands, and the boys may like to know that I called him " Dopper." He would get up the speed of a racer when after game, would stop promptly, stand perfectly steady, and the moment he saw the gun out he would just bent his neck and hold his breath until the bullet was out. He learned by experience that that was the only way to take the shock of the muzzle-loader without a bad shaking. Even if I dismounted he would stand perfectly steady. Such a horse was a treasure to any hunter and I cannot but pay this tribute to his memory.

But I am getting ahead of my story. After fully equipping myself for a hunting trip, I left Shoshong the first week in December. My companion was Phil Francis (who afterwards died on the Zambesi) and there were two Cape Colony boys with us. On arriving at the Tati I determined to search the district for elephant spoor while waiting the arrival of David Napier, with whom I had agreed to hunt. Although I started out on the 1st of January (1868) in the hope of inaugurating a prosperous new year my luck for once was out, and when I returned to the wagons five days later, I was unable to report having seen a sign of elephant spoor. However, Napier was there and when we joined our forces we had the respectable complement of 30 boys to feed, to say nothing of ourselves.

We arranged to get the wagons down to the Simbookie. We started the second week in January, all down the Tati to where the Simbookie runs into the Shashi, but there was no sign of fresh spoor and we wondered when we were going to strike their trail. Luckily we hadn't long to wait. We were having breakfast one morning, when one of the horses commenced to make a tremendous noise. My boy had him by the bridle, but he was waltzing round like a circus horse and screaming with fright. I rushed to the boy and asked him what was the matter, and for reply he pointed across the river and replied " Elephant! "

That was all I wanted to hear. I comforted and soothed the frightened horse and we then all mounted quickly, rode through the Simbookie and round a small hill, our impression being that once we got behind them they would plunge into the river and cross where we had forded. There seemed to be no other place because of the huge boulders.

However, we found it impossible to carry out our proposed manœuvre owing to the boulders, so regretfully we had to leave the herd of about 200 or so and return across the river to the place where we had saddled up.

When we got there, however, we were rewarded with a marvellous sight. For at least a mile and a half the south bank was literally black with elephants. It was impossible accurately to estimate their numbers, but there were literally thousands, and it was a spectacle of a lifetime to see the pachyderms assembled in such a mighty army. We quickly crossed over to them, and I fired the first shot to get them on the move and brought down a cow with a good pair of tusks. It was of course in the very nature of things that on this day of all days I should be short of bullets. I had started out with only eight in my pouch, for in my fondest moments I never dreamed of such mighty sport as this. However, it was no use sighing, it was time for work. Keeping close up to the herd and carefully selecting my quarry, I brought down six bulls with successive shots and then another cow.

Here I had to stop for I had travelled a considerable distance from my companions and having only one bullet left, I dared not fire that away. So I worked my way down to the Shashi and kept along the river bank for some distance, expecting to pick some of them up.

Nor was I mistaken. Napier was the first. He was in the river washing himself. I hailed him from a distance.

"Any luck, Napier?"

"Luck!" was his feeling reply, "Look at my poor————horse."

Not knowing quite what he was alluding to and thinking he must surely have had luck of some sort, I again shouted, "What luck?"

His reply was forcible, expressive and to the point, so I rode down to him. He was in a sorry plight. The skin had been taken off his face from his eye to his chin, while his eye was black and discoloured. It was clear that he had had a bad mauling of some sort. He soon explained it by saying that he had been charged and trampled by an elephant cow and both he and his horse had a bad time. It was only too obvious.

The elephant had driven its tusks right into the horse's thigh and one tusk had gone completely through the leg. From the inside wound blood was still running in a copious stream. Fortunately, I had a needle and thread with me and promptly stitched up the wound and stanched the bleeding. It was a wonder that Napier came out of this encounter alive for the elephant, he afterwards told me, had charged him from behind, had both him and his horse down and tried to stamp the life out of them. Fortunately for the horse, it was pretty fat and the elephant was unable to get a fair down blow. It was, however, able to get a purchase on the saddle and this the angry creature had trampled into a pulp, while the girth remained intact. I never saw a saddle in such a condition. It looked for all the world as though it had been chewed. Napier, after getting trampled on the shoulders and one nasty scrape down the face, managed to crawl out between the elephant's hind legs, unobserved, leaving her to expend all her rage upon the poor horse. When I saw Napier washing he was black and blue all over the shoulders, chest and back.

This was not Napier's first experience of being under a big beast. On the third day of our journey down he had been under a little black rhinoceros and was lucky to get off uninjured. Both mishaps were due to the fact that Napier was very slow, while his horse was about the same—a rather undesirable combination when big wounded animals are charging. Furthermore, Napier was not a very good rider, and his shooting was none too good. He told me that on this occasion he had put 16 bullets into one bull, without hitting a vital part.

The bull had stuck to seven or eight cows, and as Napier was following them up through the bush one of the cows must have stayed behind and gone for him.

It took us two full days to cut out and gather up the ivory I had shot. We left two boys with the horse, which we decided should not be moved for ten days, and leaving the boys, with a gun to protect themselves and the horse from lions, we followed up the elephants. We were among them until the end of March. My total bag amounted to 38 pairs of tusks while Napier got seven.

I afterwards found out from Chief Khama that this big herd of elephants had assembled somewhere low down on the Limpopo after the marula, a fruit of which they are specially fond. It appeared that towards the end of the summer, the elephants from all parts assembled for this annual fruit revel. On this occasion the Ba Mangwato got amongst them and shot one or two, starting them off. This accounted for the large herd we encountered on the Shasha.

After we had been amongst them for some time they broke up into small herds. This suited us much better for we oftener got fresh spoor than if they had remained in one body.

We also shot quite a lot of rhinoceros. They

were easy to shoot and plenty of them and as their horns weighed about 15 lbs. and were then worth something like £4, they were well worth collecting.

After this we left for the Matabele country, and reached our destination in April. I sent my ivory out by a party just going South whose wagon was not heavily loaded.

Having obtained permission from Mzilikatse to shoot in the Mashona country, we wasted no time in studying native customs or anything else, for we did not know that the Chief might not change his mind at any moment.

Before I forget it, let me here tell of one dramatic episode concerning old Mzilikatse and the attitude of the Matabele towards the missionaries that occurred on the occasion of an earlier visit in 1866. Mr. Thomas, the missionary, had invited Mzilikatse to attend divine service on a Sunday morning and to hear a short sermon.

They all agreed to go, indunas and all, and we three white men, who were staying at the King's kraal at the time—Chapman, Clark and myself— also went.

Mr. Thomas commenced in the usual way with prayer and then started his little sermon, calculated to appeal to the understanding of his Matabele hearers:

" God made the World! " he began, " God also made the Sun——"

Up sprang an excited and indignant induna. " You lie, Thomas," he shouted, " Mzilikatse made the Sun! "

There was an answering chorus of approval from the serried Matabele ranks, and the four wives who were the King's bearers promptly lifted him up and carried him from the place where his royal powers had been so severely called in question.

This attempt to convert the King and his court could hardly be called a success. The whole incident was disconcerting and unexpected, but it shows that even those barbarians had a pretty definite belief not only in the divine right but in the divine power of their kings.

We set out early in April—certainly a trifle early in view of the fever, but fortunately it did not attack me.

We got into a country that was practically unknown to white men. So far as I could learn only two white parties had ever penetrated there. The first, old John Viljoen's party, were reported to have shot 210 elephants on one trip, while the second was Mr. Hartley's party which for reasons previously explained did not get a very big bag. However, the latter party, despite their poor shooting, left the more permanent impression on the place, for the village of Hartley on the Umfulu River takes its name from this shooting party and the death there of one of the boys.

I had splendid shooting here. The elephants practically did not know what a gunshot was. On more than one occasion, I have fired at an elephant. As soon as he felt the bullet he would move off, but the others took no notice of the report; they would stand quite unconcerned until perhaps another couple of shots and the running off of two or three more wounded animals would start them all on the run. It was then that I had to work for there were elephants almost without stint and from a big-game hunter's point of view it was an ideal experience. If I had the breech-loader of to-day, I hesitate to think of the number I could have shot. You sportsmen of to-day, just imagine what it was to carry all day in the blazing sun a heavy old muzzle-loader with your powder loose in one jacket pocket, a supply of caps in another and your bullets in your pouch. Add to this that the gun " kicked " one's shoulder with almost as much force as the bullet struck the elephant, and you can believe me that it was no child's play.   In fact the recoil was so great that I was more than once knocked down by it and on two occasions I was taken completely out of the saddle.   One's shoulder was literally black and blue after a day's elephant shooting.

I had the two finest months of my life on the Umfulu on this occasion.   In all I shot 95 elephants, the ivory weighing 5,000 lbs.

CHAPTER V

WILD MAN OF THE WOODS — A WEIRD ENCOUNTER —
MZILIKATSE'S PEREMPTORY SUMMONS — A TERRIBLE
TRAGEDY—DUTCH FAMILY DECIMATED

WHILE on this trip I had a most curious experience. The history of South Africa contains
many strange stories of mysterious disappearances,
and this is another to add to the list. While we
were shooting on the Umfulu River I had gone off
alone into the bush, my boys being some distance
behind me. I had thrown myself under a tree, and
was indulging in " forty winks," when I became
aware of stealthy footsteps approaching. Accustomed to wake at the slightest sound, I sprang to
my feet with my rifle in my hand, and there, not
more than two or three yards from me, was one of
the strangest objects I have ever seen. It was certainly a white man, but such a white man! It was
a human being clothed in only the merest apology
for clothes. Such clothes as he had on were nothing but rags; his skin showed through at every
stitch, and they were held together by strips of
bark. For a hat he had the remnants of something
that had been a hat one day, but was now nothing

but a shapeless brim, from the top of which there protruded a huge shock of jet-black hair, which fell in tangled knots on his shoulders. His beard was almost indescribable. It was black like his hair, but it spread out from his face in all directions and reached almost to his waist. I have a vague idea of what Rip Van Winkle was like after his long sleep in the Catskill Mountains, and he certainly could not have presented a more uncouth appearance when he returned to his native village than did this wild man of the woods.

I at once asked him what he wanted, and who he was—at the same time keeping my gun in a convenient position. I need not have been alarmed, for the poor wretch had nothing more offensive upon him than a stick from the bush. He mouthed some gibberish, and shook his head. I tried him in Matabele, but only unintelligible answers came from him in response. At this juncture my boys came upon the scene, and I told them to try and find out something of my strange visitor. As some of the boys understood a bit of Portuguese, and he apparently knew a bit of Mashona, we ascertained at last, after much questioning, that he had been lost in the bush for about four months. He would not say where he came from, nor would he give his name, but he said he had come in from Portuguese East

Africa and had wandered in the wilderness all this time without any means of protection or anything in the way of food. It appeared that he had occasionally obtained a little food from friendly Mashonas, but for the most part had subsisted on wild fruits and berries. How he had escaped being devoured by lions I cannot understand, for he was in very dangerous country, and the feeble stick he carried in his hand was of no more protection than a garden syringe.

I tried to explain to him, through the boys and by signs, that our wagons were only a short distance behind, and that if he would go on and intercept them he would be provided with some clothes, a decent pair of boots, and a square meal, of which he apparently stood in great need. He evidently understood, for he nodded his head, and in other ways expressed his thankfulness and pleasure. He disappeared along the path we had come, whilst I and my boys proceeded on our way in the opposite direction.

When, much later in the day, the wagons caught us up I immediately enquired for my strange visitor of the morning, and was astounded to learn that he had not put in an appearance at the wagons. We never heard of him again. Whether he was a fugitive fleeing from justice, or whether he was an idiot and did not know what he was doing, is more than I can say. He flashed into my ken and floated out of it like a mote in the sunbeam—the strangest, loneliest figure it has ever been my lot to meet.

Our hunting exploits were cut somewhat shorter than we had intended, owing to the receipt of three messages from Mzilikatse to return immediately. The first we took little notice of; the second told us to come out at once if we wished to avoid trouble; while the third stated that if we did not come back without an instant's delay Mzilikatse would send and fetch us.

This was peremptory enough for us, and we accordingly decided to retrace our steps. We started to move southward early in September, but thought we could combine business with duty by having a little excursion into the fly belt[1] on our way down.

A few days before we came to this decision the boys came running to us with the news that seven bull elephants had passed in the bush close to the wagons. I went out to look at the spoor, and it was certainly good enough to warrant a trip. We followed the spoor, which went in an easterly direction, and on the following morning we came up with the elephants on a comparatively open flat. There was one large tree there, under which they had

---

Tse tse fly, whose bite is fatal to domestic animals.

taken shelter from the sun, and I was lucky enough to secure the whole seven.

It took the boys the whole of that day to chop out the ivory of six of them that I had shot comparatively close together, and on the following morning I sent two boys to chop out the ivory of the seventh, which was a considerable distance off. They left early, and after I had eaten a little breakfast I saddled up and started in their direction. As I was riding along through the high grass I saw what I took to be more elephants some distance away. There was certainly something of exceptional size moving along, but as I cautiously drew near I saw to my astonishment that it was a wagon, the top of which was covered with skins—but travelling through the high grass it had looked for all the world like a huge animal!

I rode up to it, and as I approached a woman gave expression to a perfect shriek of thankfulness, sprang out of the wagon, and ran towards me. She was a Mrs. Harrens (I am not sure of the exact spelling), an elderly Dutch lady, wife of Christian Harrens, whom I had previously met further south with the Hartley party. At the sight of me she nearly went into hysterics. She seized me in her arms, held me tightly to her, and cried as though her heart would break. For a time I could get nothing out of her, nor could she realise anything I was saying to her. She just clung on to me and cried. I could feel that there was some terrible tragedy behind it all, for she did not belong to the sentimental type that wears its heart upon its sleeve. The very fact that she was so many miles from the haunts of white men proved that she came of the hardy old voortrekker stock that feared neither loneliness nor distance. But now she had broken down completely, and it was apparent that her abandonment to grief at my appearance was the culmination of a long spell of iron-like reserve. I let her have her cry out. It was no use my attempting to stop it. She abandoned herself to her feelings, and all I could do was to utter a few words of kindly sympathy as she sobbed her heart out on my shoulder.

Gradually the sobs subsided, the tears slowly ceased, and when she had grown somewhat composed she told me of a tragedy that few women have experienced. Pointing to a little boy in the wagon, she said, " He is the only one left out of all my family! I have lost my husband, five children, and a white man by the name of Wood, who came in with us. They are all dead, and I have watched them die, one after the other! All that are left is my little boy here and this faithful native now leading the oxen. The other natives are either dead or they deserted; and just we three have been trying, God knows how many weary weeks, to get out." It appeared from subsequent conversations I had with her that after leaving the Hartley party her husband had decided to take an extended tour into the Matabele country and away to the north-west towards what is now Mashonaland. They had spent the summer there, and had been in a very sickly district during the worst period of the year. The party consisted of Harrens and his wife, three grown-up daughters, three small children, the white man Wood, and several natives. First one and then another of the party had sickened and died, and the survivors had scraped out a shallow grave and buried them there. They were all too sick to get away from the valley of death in which they were encamped, and could do nothing but wait for the end.

And the end came with terrible certainty and appalling suddenness. The two strong men, then one of the big girls, then two of the little ones, and finally the second of the big girls fell victims to the fever. Even three of the natives also succumbed, and it was at this stage only that the old lady, whose hair had grown white with grief, was forced to take control of affairs and make a desperate effort to get out alive. So she sat in the wagon all day long, and drove, while the one native who had remained with her led the oxen and did such other work at the outspan as he could.

I had a hard task to get away from her, for she was in a state of mortal fear that I would desert her, and it was pitiful to see how her nerve had broken down and how completely terrified she was of being left alone. She had kept a brave face upon it as long as she could, but once she had met a man of her own colour overwrought Nature had mercifully eased the strain, and she had practically reached the end of her courage and endurance. Of course, I assured her that I would not desert her. I left with her a Cape Colony boy, who could speak both Dutch and English, with instructions to bring the wagon down to where mine was. This he did by the second night, and on the following morning I returned.

CHAPTER VI

IN THE FLY COUNTRY—AN ELEPHANT ADVENTURE—A
LUCKY ESCAPE—THE OXEN LOST—A SEVENTY-MILE
CHASE—NAPIER'S TERRIBLE EXPERIENCE

WHEN I rejoined the wagons on the second day I found that my boy had carried out his instructions faithfully and the old lady's wagon was outspanned alongside mine. I noticed a peculiar habit she had when kraaling her oxen at night. I thought it an unnecessary thing to do, but forebore making any comment on the matter. It was a pity I did not, for if I had I should have learned that her method was the outcome of practical experience and if I had followed the same plan I should have been saved a peculiarly unpleasant adventure, and one that nearly cost me my life. But of that in its place.

One way and another I had a lot of trouble with the old lady, but there was more to come, even after we started to trek southwards. The first calamity was the breaking of the axle of her wagon. Such an accident is serious in any circumstances when travelling on the veld, but here in the heart of the Mashona country it was little short of disaster. Mrs. Harrens very nearly collapsed with despair. The thought that, after being rescued so providentially by a white man, she would again be left stranded in the bush, through the break-down of the wagon, was almost too much for her, and she was in a perfect state of terror lest I should be compelled to go and leave her. However, after considerable difficulty and hard work I was able to rig up a temporary wooden axle which answered the purpose of the real article and enabled her to continue her journey to the Transvaal.

Napier and I, having given the boys instructions to inspan on a certain day and trek southwards to the first river, the Sweswe, started separately into the fly country on foot in the hope of getting a few more elephant tusks, for although we had had a very fine bag a wagon must be very full if there is not room for a little more ivory. I was in the fly country for 14 days and had a really good time. I shot 14 bulls and 8 cows, and could have had several more cows, but refrained from shooting as the ivory in them was very light and it therefore seemed a pity to kill them.

I had one narrow squeak with an old bull in the Sweswe River, the bed of which, as many Rhodesians know, is all sand. I had two guns with me at the time and with one of them I fired at the bull at close quarters. Unfortunately it missed fire—the cap went off but the spark failed to reach the powder. I immediately handed it to my boy for him to put on another cap and in the meantime planted a bullet in the elephant with the second gun. I was watching the elephant all the time and did not notice what the boy was doing. The stupid fellow instead of putting on a fresh cap only, put in another charge of powder and a second bullet. Seeing the old elephant which I had wounded coming for me at the charge I reached out my hand for the gun, put it to my shoulder and fired.

There was a terrific explosion. The gun flew out of my hand; I saw stars and was knocked flat on my back in the river bed. For the moment I was stunned, but, promptly recovering, I sprang to my feet and saw the elephant, trumpeting with rage, nearly upon me. I tried to run but could make no headway in the loose sand while the big flat feet of the elephant enabled it to get a grip and to move almost as easily as upon solid ground. I could feel him almost on top of me and as a last resource doubled short back.

The elephant tried to do the same and as he did so gave a loud scream. I thought he had me for certain, but as I turned my head found that he had paused. In trying to turn upon me he had twisted his shoulder at the knob, just where I had lodged my bullet. It was lucky for me, for nothing could have saved me in that loose sand. As it was, the elephant was helpless, for of course he could do nothing on three legs and it did not take me long to finish him off, which I did without wasting time, thankful that I had come through such a risky experience with a safe skin.

I mentioned in an earlier experience that the elephants in those days did not know the meaning of gun fire. There were six other elephants in the river and they took not the least notice of my firing. I had four of them down before the others began to move. The fifth moved off somewhat too quickly for my liking, but eventually I brought him down and was also successful in securing the sixth.

This was an extremely lucky bag and I was sitting down on the bank of the river congratulating myself on my good fortune when I heard a tremendous din on the other side. Springing to my feet with my gun in my hand I gazed in the direction of the noise and to my surprise and amusement saw a whole host of Mashonas who had been witnesses of my shooting exploits driving an elephant towards me. They had discovered a seventh member of the herd which I had overlooked, and spreading themselves out and raising a most unearthly din they had driven the big brute to where they had heard the shooting. This was the first occasion on which I had been favoured with volunteer beaters for the noble sport of elephant hunting. It did not take long to finish the elephant off, and my Mashona friends had their share of the spoil in the shape of a goodly store of elephant meat.

Though the sport was good, this hunting in the fly country was very much like hard work, and personally I prefer the horse. The tsetse fly, as most people know, is a peculiarly vicious creature and the prompt and painful manner in which it draws blood renders it most obnoxious to human beings while of course its bite is fatal to oxen and horses.

I was in the fly country for fourteen days and got to the appointed place of meeting on a Friday, with two boys, but to my great disappointment there was no sight of the wagons. Wondering what could be the matter I sent a boy back on the trail, with instructions that as soon as he came up with the wagons he was to return, bringing with him a horse. I also started to the north behind him so as to get a mount as quickly as possible. Shortly after sunrise one of my drivers returned on horseback with a led horse accompanying him. He told a curious story which did not strike me as altogether palatable.

He said they had started according to my instructions, and outspanned the first evening. They made up a kraal in which to put the cattle, but it was of a very flimsy nature, with the result that the oxen simply walked out of it during the night and commenced grazing. This was where Mrs. Harren scored for, having tied her oxen to the yoke, she had them safe while mine and Napier's had gone off, goodness only knew where. So far as I could gather they must have been frightened soon after they got loose, and bolted, making off in the direction of the Sweswe, which they had crossed. It was quite clear that lions were after them, for I afterwards found that, on the further bank, the lions had attacked them. Five of the oxen were killed at this spot by the brutes. I followed up the spoor as rapidly as possible. The first night (Saturday) I slept close to the wagons for I found that the oxen were travelling almost in a circle. The following morning I started off about daybreak and, during the afternoon, met several of my boys returning with 16 oxen which they said they recovered amongst the Mashonas in the vicinity. The next morning I continued the search, and noticed the somewhat peculiar manner in which the oxen appeared to be crossing each other's spoor, but failed to draw any particular conclusion from it, though I afterwards was enabled to explain it. If I had realised the real meaning at the time things might have turned out differently.

At this juncture the old Matabele guide I had with me complained of hunger, and, seeing three roan antelope not far away, I was about to shoot, and felt for my powder flask to prime the nipple, but to my annoyance could not find it, and then remembered I had left it where we slept for the night. As matters transpired I was extremely foolish in not sending back for it, for its possession would have saved me and the boys much subsequent distress. As I had only the one charge in the gun I would not fire at the antelope, not knowing how useful that one charge might turn out to be, for the wise hunter never cares to be without one last shot in case of emergency.

I soon found use for it, for about sundown we saw an old rhinoceros coming down the path to the water. I got off my horse and went to meet him, halting at a very large ant-heap, which was covered with grass. As he came near the heap he gave me his side, and I raised the gun and fired, but the weapon played me a trick that the old muzzle-loaders often did in those days—it hung fire, and there was I pointing my gun at a particularly ugly and dangerous rhino. Fortunately I kept the gun straight at him, wondering for a second what was going to happen, when to my intense thankfulness the fire crept down the nipple of the gun, and the charge exploded, giving the rhino a clean shot in a vital place. He ran for about 400 yards, and then fell dead. But those old muzzle-loaders sometimes were enough to make one's hair turn grey.

We camped all night near the carcase, and I told the boys they must cut up and carry as much of the meat as possible, for I had no more powder and did not know how far we might have to go. So we started off next morning—a somewhat queer procession—each boy carrying about four to five pounds of burned meat on a stick, while I cut off a big chunk weighing perhaps 12 lbs. or more. It was lucky for me that I did so, as I should almost for a certainty have starved to death. With the usual improvidence of natives, the boys had finished the whole of their meat by next day, while I "nursed" mine carefully from the start, and my portion lasted me for some nine or ten days.

From this time followed one of the most trying experiences of my life. We again took up the spoor of the oxen on the Monday, slept upon it on the Tuesday, and on the following afternoon we came to a place where it was evident they had been lying down for several days. Once more we followed

up the spoor, and then we ascertained, what I had
suspected for some time, that they were being de-
liberately driven.   Footprints of two natives were
now plainly discernible.   It was obvious that after
the oxen crossed the river close to the outspan and
were attacked by the lions, they had been discovered
by natives, who had promptly rounded them up,
driven them across the river again at another spot,
and while I was wasting time following up the spoor
in an almost complete circle they were being driven
away to the north-east.   I could see now why the
spoors crossed each other at a particular spot.   Once
we ascertained the real meaning of things we followed hot-foot, and 70 miles from the wagons we
came up with them in a native kraal.

And what a sorry sight they presented!   When
Napier and I left them three weeks before they
were all fat and fit for the butcher.   Now, after
being worried by lions and driven to death by the
Mashonas, they were like bags of bones.   I took
possession of them without making too much fuss,
though, of course, I had my own opinion as to
whether the Mashonas were, as they said, ignorant
of the ownership of the cattle, which they had found
wandering in the bush.   It was a trying journey,
and it was sixteen days from the time I left the
wagons before I got back.   The oxen were so low

in condition that I had to give them a rest for three or four days on the Umfulu River.

When I arrived at the wagons I was amazed and startled to find that Napier had not turned up. He was now 16 days overdue, and I began to get anxious. I was compelled to move the wagons, and so soon as I got back to the oxen I inspanned, trekked through the Sweswe River, and about half a mile from the bank halted and built a strong kraal around the wagons, intending to go back in search of Napier, who had been absent now for nearly a month.

Napier was not the only one who had disappeared, leaving no trace. A little native boy of mine was missing the evening we got to the Umfulu with the oxen. The boys searched all over the country for him, but without success, and we had given him up for lost. Later on, as we were inspanning the oxen, one of the boys discovered some object on the plain, and climbing to the top of the wagon, announced excitedly that it was his long-lost little brother. He ran off to meet him, and when the poor lad reached us he was in the last stages of exhaustion. It appeared that he had completely lost himself, and had been for eight days without food, save a few wild berries. He was fearfully emaciated, but soon recovered.

I may mention here that on this wearying search for the oxen I also knew what it was to be hungry. The rhino meat lasted me for ten days, and for five days after that I did not have a scrap. The experience taught me never to leave my gun or my powder flask behind me.

I was about to start back in search of Napier in the afternoon, but something delayed my departure. This proved to be a fortunate delay, for on the following morning I had started with a dozen boys and had reached the river when we first met some of Napier's boys and then Napier himself. But it was scarcely the Napier I had left a month ago. Then a hale, hearty man. Now almost a living corpse, unable to walk and carried in a rude stretcher by four boys. He was simply racked with fever, and said he had been down with it for about 20 days. He was in a terrible way, thinking I had gone on without him, and said that that fear, more than the fever itself, had brought him almost to the verge of despair. He had had bad luck with the elephants, getting only a few cows, and, generally speaking, had no reason ever to wish to repeat the experiment of shooting through the fly country alone and on foot.

After two or three days' rest Napier had sufficiently recovered for me to make a start for the south, and after a good long trek we arrived at Inyati.

I should mention here that Mrs. Harrens continued to be of the party. She was an interesting old soul, full of quaint sayings and odd ways of looking at things.

I was talking with her one day about her husband. The dear old lady shook her head sadly as she thought of him and his sad end. She was so very, very sorry, she said, that he collapsed so quickly, " for had the dear Lord only spared him a few months longer he could have shot some more elephants, and so have provided for her in her old age! "

CHAPTER VII

DEATH OF MZILIKATSE—IN A TIGHT CORNER—IN THE
MIDST OF HOSTILE MATABELE—AN ANXIOUS TIME—
PRESENTS FOR THE INDUNA — REMINISCENCES OF
MZILIKATSE — AN INDUNA "WIPED OUT"—NAPIER'S
AMUSING ADVENTURES—END OF THE TRIP OF 1868

WE continued our journey southward as far as
the missionaries and then discovered the reason for
the urgent messages from Mzilikatse ordering us
to return. Whether the messages came from the
old Chief himself I don't know. Probably, feeling
that his end was near and being anxious that his
white friends should not be mixed up with any
disturbances that he felt would follow in connection
with his succession, he had sent for us to return so
that we might be well out of harm's way before the
storm broke. He might have been dead at the time
and these were messages from the Council of Chiefs
in his name. At any rate the rumour of his death
was in everyone's mouth, the whole countryside was
in a state of uproar, and with the old man's tight
hand removed and with no chief appointed to take
the restless spirits in hand, there was a tendency
towards outrage and plunder which boded ill for
our little party.

We had seen signs of restlessness for some time,

but the first real breath of danger reached us at
the kraal where I first saw Mzilikatse on my first
trip into the country with Mr. Chapman. It was
at the Bembesi, Ingubo being the induna. As the
wagons came to the kraal, about two thousand
Matabele surrounded us, with threatening gestures.
They first seized our boys, stripped them of all their
clothing and gave one or two of them a severe beat-
ing with sticks and knobkerries. A vast number of
them were armed with assegais and these swarmed
up close to us, placed their spears against the wagon
sides, and apparently only waited for the signal to
fall upon us and " eat us up " in true Matabele
fashion.

It was an anxious moment or two. I was sitting
in front, on the wagon box, trying to appear as
unconcerned as possible, but inwardy feeling that
I had certainly experienced more comfortable
moments in my career. I was wondering what sort
of a miracle would happen to get us out of a very
nasty corner when to my joy I saw Ingubo the
induna. I recognised him at once and he was not
easily to be mistaken. It was the same short, squat,
square, light-coloured Kafir* I had seen years ago. I
had only seen him during the first few months' stay
at his kraal but thinking the best thing I could do
was to put on a bold face, I jumped from the wagon,

---

* Kafir, a native.

pushed my way through the serried ranks of the warriors and walked up to him, holding out my hand, with the greeting, " How are you, Ingubo? "

He seemed a trifle nonplussed, apparently had no recollection of me and asked me who I was.

I quickly told him how we had met in the same kraal some years before, recalled various incidents to his mind and without giving him time to make a counter move I invited him to come up to the wagon as I had a very nice present for him.

I could see by his eyes that his desire for a present overcame all other considerations, and, motioning back the reluctant braves, he followed me to the wagon and climbed up in front with me. In the tent of the wagon I had a bundle of lovely blue-crane feathers hanging up. It was a really fine bundle, weighing 1½ lbs. to 2 lbs., and I knew that these feathers were prized above everything by the natives for purposes of adornment. Hastily cutting the bundle down from the tent, I ripped through the cord that bound them, and spread the delicate plumes all along the seat. I saw his eyes glisten with pleasure as he saw such a treasure unfolded, and I gathered them into a bundle and handed them to him.

The old fellow received them in his arms, and hastily commenced to get down, but his precipitancy to get away made me still doubtful of his pacific intentions, and I at once checked him and intimated that I had something more for him.

He paused, and I played my final card. Picking up a bar of lead 12 lbs. in weight—I was stronger in those days than I am to-day—I held it out in one hand. He took it unsuspectingly, but the weight was too much for him, and he dropped it to the floor of the wagon. With a smile I handed it back to him, put another of the same weight on top of it, and the old man, literally as well as metaphorically overloaded with gifts, scrambled down. I guessed rightly that the lead would " clinch " his friendship, for lead, powder and guns were the most prized articles that one could give to the natives in those days—particularly lead, which, on account of its weight, was even less readily obtainable than powder.

The old induna dropped to the ground grunting his appreciation, and, with a few sharp words, ordered the impatient warriors to fall back, saying that I was his friend. They drew back at once from the wagon, leaving Ingubo near me.

" Where are you going to outspan, white man? " he asked.

I replied that I proposed to make camp down by the river (the Bembesi).

"All right," he replied, looking me meaningly in the face. " But do not stay too long."

I took the hint, and, as fast as I could, without showing undue signs of fear, I not only put the Bembesi but as big a strip of territory as I could between Ingubo's kraal and myself.

I afterwards learned that when Lobengula became chief he " wiped out " Ingubo and his kraal to a man. The massacre was complete, for Ingubo had been opposed to Lobengula's succession, holding that Kuruman was the rightful heir. I, too, believe that Kuruman was the legitimate successor, but he could not be found, and Lo Ben, therefore, was chosen to the chieftainship, an honour which he proceeded to celebrate in true savage fashion by " eating up " all who had failed to support him from the outset.

It is somewhat out of its chronological order, but I am reminded by this incident at Ingubo's kraal of a curious experience I had here on the occasion of my first visit. I mentioned, in an earlier chapter, Mzilikatse's order to his people to capture alive a big crocodile which had devoured a child. My personal experience showed me that Mzilikatse regarded certain animals with peculiar veneration. I have previously said that with every white man in the Matabele country was a guide, who was, in other words, a spy—sometimes a very decent fellow, sometimes not. It was lucky that mine was of the first-named variety, or I might have got into trouble. One day I was on the banks of the river overlooking a clear pool, the floor of which was literally covered with white bones—mostly rhinoceros bones, so far as I could see, but many others of a smaller and more suggestive size. On a sand bank were several big, ugly crocodiles, and the sight of them and that aquatic sepulchre filled me with disgust and rage. Raising my gun I sighted on the biggest of the saurians, and finished him off with a bullet through his brain. Just as I did so my guide glided out from the shadow of a tree and touched me on the shoulder.

"Don't kill any more," he said, with a curious look in his eyes. "Mzilikatse does not allow any of them to be shot. He says that the crocodiles and the wolves must not be killed—that they have to live just as we have. Other things you may kill, but not crocodiles and wolves; they are sacred. If I were to tell Mzilikatse there would be trouble, but as you are a young man and did not know, I will not tell him this time."

Just one more story of Mzilikatse before resuming. Chapman told me that on the trip he made

into the Matabele country, the year before I first
went in with him, Mzilikatse had agreed to purchase a wagon from him. The old chief came down
to the outspan to take possession of his purchase,
bringing with him the agreed amount of ivory which
was to be handed over in exchange. Chapman was
not expecting him so quickly, and had not off-
loaded the wagon with his trade goods, provisions,
etc. This he at once commenced to do, whereupon
Mzilikatse, obviously very much annoyed, shouted
out—

" What are you taking the inside of that wagon
out for? When I sell you a bullock I don't take its
inside out before handing it over."

It took some time to mollify the old man, and to
convince him that a wagon was a " wagon," and not
a wagon with all its contents.

But, to resume. Trekking south, the spirit of
unrest and insolence was manifest on every hand.
Going past one kraal a lot of young Matabele
turned out and walked by the side of the wagons,
clearly up to mischief. Napier at the time was
riding on my wagon with me. The young scoundrels
got into Napier's wagon, which was behind mine,
seized his feather mattress and pillow, ripped them
open, and darted off with the coverings, which they

wanted for "limbo." The first thing we noticed was the swarm of little black, yelling rascals disappearing in a moving cloud of white feathers. Napier's language as he gave chase after his beloved feather-bed was quite equal to the occasion, but he had to content himself with half a wagon-load of feathers, while the remainder, also the coverings, trailed away into the bush.

This was not the only experience we had with those impish youngsters hereabouts. It was at this spot (crossing the Kokwee, near Thaba's induna) that I was very much amused at another incident in which Napier got the worst of it.

I should mention that Napier had developed a partiality for Kafir beer, and, while I was busy with some wagon repairs, Napier improved the shining hour by producing a basket of beads and other goods fascinating to the native mind and announcing to the gaping and inquisitive native youngsters who came prying round that he was open to do business— beads for beer. The glad tidings soon spread and presently the lads came along with calabashes of beer, escorted by their dusky sweethearts who fingered the beads and the gaudy trinkets with all the fine criticism of a society lady in an Oxford Street jewellery establishment. However, business was soon in fine progress. Napier sat in the shadow of the wagon with his basket of trade goods on his knees and two or three buckets around him. As each transaction was completed the beer was poured into the buckets, and the beads, etc., were handed over. So it went on until Napier had filled the buckets with beer, and had also secured a goodly supply of Kafir corn, wherewith to make a further supply, for, being still weak after his fever he felt that he needed plenty of nourishment.

Suddenly, and without a word of warning, the basket containing the balance of the beads was snatched off his legs by some enterprising youngster, others seized the buckets of beer, and before poor Napier, who was still very shaky, could rise to his feet and chase them they were on the other side of the river and there they sat and drank the beer, laughed at us and mocked us with the beads. Much as I felt inclined to chastise the young varlets, I could not help laughing heartily at Napier's impotent wrath at being so completely outwitted when he had looked forward to such a glorious drink.

It was at this spot that I had a good deal of trouble with Mrs. Harrens's wagon. After telling the boys to inspan I went on ahead on horseback, hoping to shoot some meat for the pot that evening. I was lucky enough to sight a herd of giraffe, and turned a fat cow on to the road, where I shot it.   As the wagons did not come on as expected, I returned along the road, and found that the axle of the old lady's wagon had this time completely collapsed.   She was in a fury of despair and rage—despair that I would now certainly leave her in the lurch; rage at the rottenness of the wagon.   She expressed her opinion of the man who sold the wagon to her husband in terms that should have made his ears burn, though he were a thousand miles away.   When she concluded her opinions of him with a wish that she would like to see him with the point of the axle balanced on his nose, and she after him with an ox-sjambok, and she would teach him to humbug a poor widow woman, I smiled serenely, for the man who sold the wagon was " Big Phillips," popularly known as the " Playful Elephant," who could have taken both myself and the dear old vrouw, one in each hand, and thrown us on to the top of the wagon.

Sending some of the boys on to cut up the giraffe, I chopped down a good pole, placed it under the broken axle, and tied it to the side of the wagon.   In this way we got to the Umgusa, where next day I put in a false wooden axle, which lasted the remainder of the journey.

Early that morning I saw fresh elephant spoor below the drift, and quickly saddled up and got the elephants just above where Bertlesen's lime-kilns now stand. The bush was very thick, and I only got one shot, but this brought down a young bull with tusks weighing about 25 lbs. each. I did not then know that the country was more open further on, or I should have followed up, but as the spoor indicated that they were a poor lot I returned to the wagons. Next morning I sent my formal farewell greetings to Mzilikatse at old Bulawayo, only a few miles away (I did not go in to see if he were alive or dead), and made tracks as quickly as I could for the south.

I did not stop, except for the usual outspans, until I reached the Ramaquabane River, where I waited for some Boers who had gone into the Zambesi country with a quantity of goods I had advanced to them on credit, the stipulation being that they should pay me in ivory.

Old Mrs. Harrens went on, while Napier proceeded to Shoshong. I remained on the Ramaquabane for three weeks, and had a most laughable and enjoyable time. Old Jan Lee and his family had settled here. Jan had built a comfortable house and they certainly were having a happy time. The fun consisted in hearing the old man talk. He would tell the most circumstantial yarns, full of adventure and humour, by the hour together, and to listen to him you would think he had left no elephants in the country. At the same time his son would be whispering to me that his father was a second edition of Baron Münchausen, that he was too frightened to go near an elephant, that he had never shot one and was never likely to shoot one. But the gravity of the old man in telling adventures and the bursts of Homeric laughter that invariably followed their recital kept the house in a constant state of merriment.

The Boers I was waiting for turned up at last and handed me over a rare lot of ivory. It was lucky for me that I had sent mine down by Napier or I should not have been able to find transport for it. However, I now had plenty of room, started for the South with my load, and reached Shoshong early in November, where I met my brother Harry who had come up with Francis. I went on to Shechillies, sold by ivory—between 11,000 and 12,000 lbs. in weight, which I had both traded and shot—and got drafts for same on Port Elizabeth at an all-round price of 6s. 10½d. per lb.

CHAPTER VIII

WITH THE ELEPHANTS AGAIN — A TRIP WITH CHIEF KHAMA—HUNGRY CAMP FOLLOWERS—GIFFORD CHASED BY AN ELEPHANT—A USELESS GUN — WE LOSE OUR BEARINGS — A TROPICAL THUNDERSTORM—SOME NARROW RISKS

THE life of an elephant hunter had by this time completely fascinated me, and, returning to Shoshong, I decided to go into the hunting grounds once more. The young chief Khama—who had not only heard of my exploits with the gun but had seen my big loads of ivory—said he would go in with me. My brother also decided to accompany me, together with a gentleman named Gifford. It took some little time to make our arrangements, but by the end of the year we got away and were in the elephant country in January, 1869. The exact locality was about 100 miles above the Tuli. Here I remained for full three years, on and off, sending out my ivory from time to time, and the only occasions upon which I went out were when my boys wanted to go home and have a rest and I had to go out and get a fresh supply of boys, food supplies, ammunition, etc.

89

The expedition was not very successful while Khama was with us, owing to so much time being taken up with shooting " for the pot." He had an enormous crowd of followers with him—some three hundred or more—and as they brought no food with them and trustfully looked to our guns to provide them with a daily supply of fresh meat we had all our work cut out to keep the larder replenished, without devoting ourselves to more profitable game. Fortunately Khama did not stop long, and we certainly were not sorry when this gigantic native picnic came to an end. The fact of the matter was that Khama was getting nervous. There had always been a dispute about the territory under the control of Mzilikatse and the Bechuanas. The piece of territory between the Macloutsie and the Tuli Rivers was, so to speak, neutral territory, both nations claiming it as their country, but neither making any definite attempt to assert sovereignty over it. But we were shooting well inside the Matabele country, and Khama knew that it was decidedly unsafe for him to be there, for the Matabele would have stood no nonsense with regard to a neighbouring ruler " trespassing " in their undisputed country. So he decided to return, and departed southwards, taking with him his huge *entourage,* and their ravenous appetites!

After this we had some good sport, and steady shooting, but Gifford did not do too well, though he was a fair shot and decent rider. The only reason I can advance for his non-success was his over-cautiousness and the use of a worn-out gun. I proved the last-mentioned point in a very convincing manner. One day we came up with a large number of elephants, and all of us commenced firing and followed up the herd as they got on the run. Naturally, after a time we became separated. Following up my own line I brought down two young bulls—one of which, however, got up and completely disappeared—and after this four cows, all close together. A large buck sail would have covered the whole of them as they fell. Just as I had dropped the last I heard Gifford shouting close by, and then an elephant trumpeting as though chasing something. I listened anxiously and moved in the direction of the sounds. My fear that the " hunter " had become the " hunted " was only too true. Gifford first came into view, running, and said that an elephant was after him. He said he had shot at it and wounded it, that it had turned upon him and prevented him from shooting at any of the others, or even getting near them. In fact it was chasing him " off the property," so to speak. As I had finished my supply of bullets I asked him how he was off and he replied that he had plenty. I offered to take his gun—his bullets were not suitable for my gun—and give him half of what I shot. He readily agreed and we started after them again. Soon we saw one, but more than a mile away. We started to get in front of him and after a good long gallop we dismounted, loosened the girths of our saddles to give our horses a blow and then climbed a tree to get a better view. We could see all around for a considerable distance, but, curiously enough, there was nothing to be seen but bush. We remained in the tree for quite ten minutes, but there was no sign of anything moving, so Gifford got down, tightened the girths of his saddle preparatory to making a move and I called to him to do the same for me. I climbed down, Gifford had already mounted, and I was about to do the same when only a few yards away I saw the elephant moving. I rushed to Gifford for his gun, and fired a shot that would, I thought, prevent the elephant from going very far. I was mistaken as to this, however, for he continued to move away, for all the world as though he had not been hit. It will scarcely be credited, but I fired ten more shots at him and then, tired with useless firing, I handed the gun to Gifford who put in four more bullets. Even with all this lead in him the elephant very nearly stole a march upon us. We were sitting on our horses close to him, expecting every minute to see him drop dead, when he turned savagely upon us and rushed after Gifford for some hundred yards. Then the poor brute sat down on his hind-quarters, gave one loud scream, and rolled over dead. He had a fine pair of tusks, each weighing about 60 lbs. Naturally we were curious to know how he had managed to survive for so long our fusillade of lead, for I was certain that my own bullets had taken effect, and I was equally sure that Gifford had found the mark. I had told Gifford that his gun was no good when I handed it back to him, and now I proved it by cutting out some of the bullets. The majority had penetrated not more than six inches, and in some cases not more than three, so the gun was obviously unfitted to kill animals some four feet through. The gun was a well-made one, but it had been in use so long that the rifling had completely worn out.

We returned to the wagons on the Saturday with a nice little lot of ivory, for, in addition to those I had already shot, I was lucky to get a solitary old bull who had evidently been roaming by himself for a long time, having probably been turned out of the herd. The old bachelor's tusks weighed about 90 lbs. each.

We made a fresh start on the Monday, on this

occasion being accompanied by my brother Harry.
We had a very curious experience. It was very
cloudy the day we started and we did not see the
sun for four days. Heavy rain clouds were sweep-
ing in from the east and the result was that we
entirely lost our bearings and at times were completely at a loss to know in which direction we were
going. On one occasion we came to a river where,
according to our ideas, the water was running the
wrong way. We were all suffering under the same
delusion, and though we knew in our own minds
that the law of gravity had not been suddenly sus-
pended on this occasion, merely to add to our per-
plexities, we could not rid ourselves of the idea that
the whole scheme of things was, somehow, wrong.
However, leaving the delusion to take care of itself,
we came across the spoor of a very large herd of
elephants and started in pursuit. This was on a
Wednesday; we followed on it all day, picked it
up again the following morning, and kept to the
trail all day. It was very dark, with every appearance of torrential rains falling at any moment. We
were still in complete ignorance as to our exact
whereabouts, or the direction in which we were
travelling, but as the spoor was now getting very
fresh we determined to run all risks and to get up to
our quarry with the least possible delay. We passed

a cow that had recently calved and, carefully getting to leeward of her so that she should not alarm the others, worked round to come up to close quarters with the herd.

My brother got on to some spoor on the top side of the wind. I called out to him several times to come back, warning him that, if the elephants winded us, they would bolt and we should not get them, and that our only chance was to keep to the leeward. He took no notice, however, and went on in what seemed to me a somewhat obstinate manner, especially seeing that he had had no previous experience of elephant hunting. Just about this time the rain that had been threatening for several days began to fall. Those who know anything of a Rhodesian rainfall at its best, or rather worst, will not need to be told what happened. The rain came down in sheets, in buckets-full if you like, not in drops, but in solid spouts of water, blotting out all view of the bush and making it utterly impossible for us to go on. Gifford and I got off our horses, took off our saddles, huddled up together on the top of a small ant-heap with the saddles on our heads, and there we sat like two drowned rats, with the rain shooting off the saddles in spouting streams on either side of us! As showing the extent of the rainfall, in ten minutes the water on the level ground around us was quite four inches deep.

It cleared up at length, the sun shone and at last we were able to locate ourselves; but, unfortunately, it was within half-an-hour of sundown so we pitched camp for the night. At twilight we heard five shots in the distance and some time later my brother came into camp, saying he had run up some bull elephants and had fired the five shots at them, without effect. We had a decidedly wet and uncomfortable night, but we soon forgot the discomfort on the following morning when the sun shone gloriously and the rich scent of the moistened bush and earth reached our nostrils.

We mounted and very quickly picked up fresh elephant spoor. There were only three animals, it was true, but as the spoor was very large I anticipated getting big ivory. Imagine my disgust when, after travelling some considerable distance, I discovered I had left my powder with my boys at the camp. Telling Gifford and my brother to continue on the spoor I returned to camp, got my powder and returned. On the way I saw a beautiful sight. About 50 giraffe were moving along slowly in front of me; they would move a few paces, then pause and stand still, looking about them. I surmised from this that the elephants were not far off, and in this I was quite correct for old " Dopper," who took little notice of giraffes, suddenly pricked up his ears and, following the direction of his glance, I saw an elephant coming across my front. I quietly got up alongside and put in a good shot. He started off at a gallop and as I quickly reloaded, another one came along quite close to me. I had one foot in the stirrup at the time and was just swinging over old " Dopper's " back when that intelligent creature, not at all appreciating such close quarters, jumped away with a frightened snort, swinging me up against a lovely *wacht-ein-beitje* bush, whose thorns caught my clothing and pulled me violently to the ground. Happily, the elephant swerved at this acrobatic exhibition and I managed to crawl well out of sight, till I reached my horse.

Just as I mounted again my brother and Gifford came up, having heard the report of my gun, and as the elephant had disappeared we galloped off as hard as we could for some hills in the distance, the three of us ranging about 400 yards apart. In this way I ran up against one big elephant, brought him down with two shots and immediately heard a trumpeting of a large number of elephants right ahead—in fact the whole country appeared to be swarming with them. The elephant I had brought down was not the one I had previously fired at, for although this one had a splendid pair of tusks I knew that the other had much bigger ivory. This I afterwards proved, for some Bushmen discovered him some three days afterwards, quite dead, and I had to pay them three muskets and a quantity of power, lead, and caps for the ivory. It was worth it, however, for the tusks weighed no less than 250 lbs. That was the heaviest ivory I had secured in any of my trips, and I may say here that it constituted a record so far as I am concerned.

Following up the sound of the trumpeting I heard several shots from my companions and, quickly getting on to the spoor, I was lucky enough to bring down five more bulls, none of them under 40 lbs. per tusk.

In my next instalment I will tell of how my brother got lost in the bush for nine days and was nearly starved to death.

CHAPTER IX

LOST IN THE BUSH—MY BROTHER'S TERRIFYING EXPERI-
ENCE—SAVED BY BUSHMEN—A HUNTER'S QUALIFICA-
TIONS—VISITS FROM LIONS—A DOUBLE FRIGHT—PAN-
DEMONIUM IN CAMP

I CONTINUED after the elephants for the best part
of the day and it was late in the afternoon before I
and Gifford came together again. He did not appear to have had much luck, only one cow having
fallen to his gun. Goodness knows what he had
been doing, for the elephants were plentiful enough
and I had secured a big bag. As we knew it would
take at least two days to cut out and collect the
ivory, we decided to pitch camp. Sundown came
but there were no signs of my brother so I fired
several shots to let him know our whereabouts. He
fired one in reply, but it was a long way off, and
though I knew it would take him some time to reach
us I had no anxiety on his behalf. As Gifford said
his cow was close at hand I went to have a look at
it, taking two boys with me to cut off the trunk, as
all the axes were in use by the boys who were cutting
out the ivory from the elephants I had shot. We
accordingly removed the trunk but when I again

reached camp, finding an axe there, I sent the boys back to the cow and told them to chop out the tusks. They returned late that night with the ivory and mentioned the curious fact that when they reached the elephant the second time they noticed that some-one had cut a large piece of meat out of the shoulder, though there was nothing to show whose handiwork it was.

We waited up late that night for my brother, but there was no sign of him. Early next morning I fired several more shots in the hope of attracting his attention and enabling him to discover our where-abouts, but got no answering shot in return.

By this time I was genuinely alarmed for his safety and immediately set off in the direction of the shot we had heard the previous evening. I picked up his horse's spoor close to the spot where the remains of Gifford's cow were lying. I followed it for some distance and then to my horror found his saddle and bridle completely torn to pieces by wolves.[1] The spoor of the horse continued, however, but we could see that it was knee-haltered and had been grazing slowly along. We followed the horse's spoor the whole of that day till nightfall and then were compelled to camp for the night. Unfortu-nately there was a heavy rain during the night which obliterated all spoor, and as we were totally unable

[1] Hyenas.

to pick it up in the morning there was nothing for
me to do but to return to the camp. Gifford by
this time had collected all the ivory and we at once
retraced our steps to the wagons, which were outspanned on the Shasha. On our way Gifford got
two more elephants and I got four bulls. Leaving
the boys to cut out the ivory we hurried on to the
wagons and there, to my great joy, was the long-
lost brother who had arrived on the previous day,
having been separated from us for nine days. He
had been brought into camp by some Bushmen who
found him some 80 miles from the wagons. They
were very good to him and gave him a feed of dry
mealies, not much for a starving man, but it was all
they had. These dry mealies constituted his only
food for the whole nine days, with the exception of
a meercat, which he had run down. He said the
flesh was delicious! It appeared that he was the
person who had cut a piece of flesh from the shoulder
of Gifford's cow—though he said the meat was so
tough he could not eat it—and when I asked him
how in the world he could have lost himself after
being so close to us, he said it was due to his horse.

He had off-saddled fairly close to the elephant
and could actually hear the boys talking and cutting out the ivory when he noticed that his horse
had strayed out of sight. He immediately sprang

up and tried to find it but it had disappeared, where-upon he put his saddle and bridle in a bush for safety and tried to find us. He got back to the cow again but the tusks had by this time been removed and the boys were gone. At this calamity he got into a flurry, and lost his head. Anyone who has ever had the misfortune to be " bushed " will realise his sensa-tions. He wandered on in the direction he thought we would be, but, as might be expected in the cir-cumstances, he was going away from us all the time.

When I asked him why he did not fire his gun and let us know where he was, he said he tried to discharge it but, to add to his distress, found that the powder had got wet the previous day and it was not until nearly dark that he was able to dry it. It was then that he had fired the shot we heard. Even then, however, he was unable to locate us so he de-cided to make tracks, as nearly as possible, for the wagons, and trusted to his good fortune to be able, by keeping to the east all the time, to come up with them.

He slept or rather " rested " in trees at night—for it is not easy to sleep in a tree—and during the day anxiously pushed on, worn out by hunger, anxiety and lack of sleep. He was in a bad way when the Bushmen picked him up, as before stated, and there was never a more thankful man than he to receive a few dry mealies from the bush barbarians.

That finished his elephant hunting. He had received too much of a fright ever to go off into the trackless bush again. He thought elephant hunting was a fine sport for those who could find their way by instinct through the bush, but it was not good enough for him who was not so blessed.

I never expected to see the horse again but, to my surprise, came across him about two months afterwards in the possession of some Bushmen, who found him wandering about. His knees were very sore from the continuous knee-haltering but he was otherwise none the worse, and though I paid the Bushmen handsomely for finding and taking care of him, he was worth it. I subsequently sold him at a good profit and he turned out to be a first-class hunting-horse.

With reference to my brother's experience I may say that the hunter's craft is not picked up in a day, especially as regards elephant shooting. One needs to be very observant of everything around one so as to be able to locate one's-self at almost any moment. Some people quickly get flurried, especially if suddenly aroused from sleep, and do not seem to be able to collect their senses for some minutes. Personally when I was aroused at any time of the night all my senses were alert in a second, and I could tell the time within a few minutes, while it goes without saying that if I had not been gifted with a keen sense of " locality " and able to find my way through the bush unhesitatingly I could not have followed up and subsequently relocated the elephants I had shot. In fact, with the exception of those days, previously mentioned, when we did not see the sun for days, I do not remember ever having lost the sense of direction.

Another point for the successful hunter is that he must be able to track game himself. This is more than half the battle, for if he has to trust entirely to his native boys in this respect, he may expect to be finely humbugged by them in all sorts of ways. They will lose a spoor purposely, or take a wrong spoor if it suits them and they want to get back to camp. But once find a spoor making in the direction of the wagons and, though they may have been listless enough before, they will be as keen as a razor-blade, especially if you have been out for a few days without getting on to fresh spoor.

After all, the natives are very human and in view of the hard times they sometimes experience it is no wonder they resort to dodges to avoid too much exertion. Theirs is by no means an easy, pleasant or safe task. When out with a hunter

they frequently have to be out all night in all kinds
of weather, sometimes in drenching rain with nothing to keep them dry, wood too wet to burn and
with the constant fear that a lion or some other
animal may be on the lookout for supper. Many
a black boy has been snapped up in this way, for
lions are very bold and are not always deterred by
a fire, while other denizens of the forest are capable
of giving one a fright, if nothing worse.

I remember once, we were making a camp for
the night. It was quite dusk, but the horses were
still grazing under the charge of a Cape boy. Suddenly he shouted, " Bring the gun, baas, bring the
gun." I immediately ran to him and he pointed
to a big male lion not many yards away, the brute
evidently contemplating an attack either upon the
horses or the boy. It was so dark I could scarcely
see the sight on my gun, but I fired and the bullet
just missed the lion, knocking up the dust all round
his neck. With an angry growl he made off.

We secured the horses as quickly as possible,
made up some big fires all around us, and after
eating the evening meal settled ourselves comfortably to sleep, Gifford, myself and the Colony boy
being at one fire together. I was awakened by
hearing the horses snorting and knew that this por-

tended the presence of danger.   Hastily rising to
my knees, I peered over a small bush that we had at
our heads and looked—straight into the face of a
big lioness who was not more than six feet away!
She had been taking a quiet survey of the camp by
the light of the fires and, evidently, when I popped
up my head she got as big a fright as I did, and
promptly bolted, leaving behind her a peculiarly
offensive odour which compelled us to shift our
quarters and kept us awake for some time.

It was about three hours later, and we were
just sleeping comfortably again, when there was
another scare.   The fire was suddenly scattered all
over the place, there was a fearful grunting noise,
the horses screamed with terror and snapped their
reims, the boys with howls of fear climbed the
nearest trees and the whole camp was a perfect
pandemonium.   The cause of all this trouble was a
pugnacious little black rhinoceros who, undismayed
by our fire, just blundered through it in his own
pig-headed way right into our midst and nearly
frightened us to death.   He was probably startled
at the noise his little exploit evoked, for within a
minute he had scuttled away into the darkness.

We had considerable difficulty in catching the
horses.   The poor creatures were very restless after

this second trial of their nerves in one night and we had great trouble in pacifying them. They were almost frightened to death and as by this time everybody's nerves were more or less shaken, further sleep, by tacit consent, was out of the question. The boys piled more wood on the fires and we promptly made ourselves a kettle of coffee and sat by the fire drinking till daybreak.

CHAPTER X

MR. HARTLEY'S PARTY AGAIN—A LION ADVENTURE—THE
HEAD-MAN SEIZED—MY EXPLOIT WITH AN ASSEGAI—
A RISKY UNDERTAKING—COWARDICE OF NATIVES—
TWO PLUCKY PICANNINS—THEIR FIGHT WITH A LION

As soon as it was light we moved off and, picking up the spoor of elephant, we started in pursuit.
They took us a long way up the Ramaquabane
River, the trail crossing the main road. We were
somewhat surprised to find at this spot several
wagons outspanned. These proved to be old Mr.
Hartley's, but there were only native boys in charge
at the time, the white men having also gone in
pursuit of elephant. The presence of white men
was too rare an occurrence for us to miss the chance
of meeting them, so we left the elephants we were
pursuing to their own devices, off-saddled and
waited for my old friends to turn up. This they
did eventually and, after renewing old acquaintance,
told us that they had been unsuccessful in their particular jaunt that day but had shot a rhinoceros not
very far from the camp and had left a number of
boys there to cut out the eatable part and bring it
along as food.

We had many reminiscences to exchange, and just as we were full of talk one of Mr. Hartley's boys came running up at full speed, crying and moaning and in a state of considerable distress. For a time it was difficult to get a coherent story out of him, but eventually we calmed him down and he then told us, with many gesticulations, that the head-man had been seized by a lion, killed and carried off into the reeds in spite of their attempts to save him.

Upon hearing this startling news we immediately sprang to our feet, caught our horses, saddled up, and with the boy racing ahead of us to show us the way, we galloped for the scene of the tragedy. We had not gone more than half way when we saw a procession coming towards us.

Leading the way was the " dead " man—walking, with a boy on either side supporting him. He wasn't quite dead; in fact he was worth half-a-dozen dead men, but there was no doubt that he had received a very bad mauling. Upon questioning him and his comrades it appeared that, being too lazy to come back by the proper path, they had taken a short cut through some river reeds, when the lion came upon the scene from behind. The king of beasts, attracted probably by the smell of the rhinoceros meat, and being in search of supper, made a spring and—caught the head-man, bending. There were four ugly wounds, the marks of His Majesty's four big teeth in the head-man's anatomy, but beyond the fact that he was unable to sit down for some weeks he was very little the worse.

After being bowled over in this undignified fashion and hauled away for a short distance, it appeared that the head-man's struggles, and the other boys' shrieks, had scared the lion sufficiently for him to release his victim, who now, with much circumstantial detail and appropriate gesture, accompanied by innumerable groans, told us how the tragic affair had happened. It took some time to tell, naturally, for though the lion went straight for the mark, no native ever yet lived who could do the same, when telling anything that happened. He had to begin at the beginning and wander all round the subject, in which he was aided and abetted by his comrades, and by the time they had finished we had had the whole scene re-enacted before our eyes and knew what every man said, thought, or did, together with their opinions of the lion and his dastardly and cowardly method of attack.

Eventually, the indaba was finished, and we proceeded to the spot where the rumpus had occurred. Our dogs were with us but we could not induce them to go into the reeds where the lion had taken refuge. We were determined to get the lion, but when the dogs refused to go in, there was no anxiety on the part of anyone to make a move.

Seeing that they were all diffident I, rather rashly perhaps, said I would go in, provided they all stood by with their guns ready. This they agreed to do, and as a gun was useless in a close encounter I handed my gun to one of the boys and armed myself with the big assegai that the head-man had dropped.

I dropped down the bank into the thick reeds, and at the second stride I trod upon something which gave a loud scream. In an instant I stabbed with the assegai with all my might and, drawing back the weapon, found I had impaled a young lion cub, about six weeks old. The lioness, doubt-less frightened by the noise of our big party, was afraid to come back and protect her offspring. This was certainly fortunate so far as I was con-cerned, for she would unquestionably have given me a very rough time.

At the sight of the cub the dogs plucked up courage and came into the reeds with me. They smelled out and killed two more cubs, but the parents were not to be found.

We returned to Mr. Hartley's wagons and

slept there that night.   On the following morning
we set off along the bank of the river, and off-
saddled, while it was yet early, by the side of a
small spruit.   We made a fire, grilled some of the
rhino meat and, having satisfied our keen appetites, stretched ourselves out in the warm morning
sunlight, filled our pipes and prepared to enjoy
a blissful ten minutes.

We were in the midst of a delightful reverie
that the huntsman-smoker knows so well, when my
day-dreams were suddenly dispelled by Gifford,
who quietly touched me on the arm and pointed to
a buffalo cow which was grazing not more than a
hundred yards away from us.   We kept perfectly
still for a few seconds, but just as we were about
to move we heard a fierce growl, saw a flash of a
tawny something—and the buffalo cow was rolling
over in the middle of a great cloud of dust.

The whole thing happened in a flash.   Almost
before we had recovered from our astonishment the
dust had cleared away and we could see a big male
lion and lioness savagely tearing at the buffalo.

Our guns were lying by our side, and it did not
take us many seconds to agree as to which each of
us should take.   Within five seconds our guns had
spoken, and both lions were lying dead by the side
of their victim.   Reloading, we walked over to the

three dead bodies and ascertained that it was the lion that had made the first assault. He had jumped squarely on the shoulders of the buffalo, and, holding onto the neck by one paw he had put the other over the buffalo's nose, thrust in his great claws, and broken the poor beast's neck with one mighty twist.

We looked around to see where our boys were, but, as usual when lions were about, they had deemed discretion the better part of valour, and were all of them in the topmost branches of the nearest trees. We shouted to them to come down, but they were mighty reluctant to do so. The cowards said they were afraid of something else turning up, and they were not coming down until they were sure that all danger was past.

Perhaps the cowardice of natives in such circumstances is excusable, for there have been tragedies enough among them, plenty of whom have fallen victims to the lions.

There was one very plucky feat, however, I remember, performed by two young Matabele boys, and it deserves to be placed on record, for it is one of the finest pieces of bravery on the part of two lads that I have ever heard. These picannins were herding cattle one day. It was in the wet season, there was a nasty drizzling rain, obscuring all the

landscape, save for an immediate twenty yards or
so. Suddenly two lions came on the scene, sprang
on to a cow and killed it. This stampeded the remainder of the cattle, while the two terrified boys,
with shouts of terror, ran madly behind the panic-
stricken herd.

Gradually, however, the boys recovered from
their panic, and stopped to talk it over. Solemnly
they debated the whole matter—and here comes in
a beautiful illustration of pride of race—and they
said: " We are Matabele boys; we are the sons of
brave men; the Matabele do not fear lions, and because we are Matabeles we must not be afraid. If
we went back to the kraal and told our people we
were frightened by lions, they would laugh at us,
and say we would never be Matabele warriors, but
were only ' girls,' and only fit to stay with women
in the kraals. And so we should be laughed at all
our lives. We must go back and kill the lions."

It sounds incredible, but those plucky boys returned. They crept cautiously through the bush
until they came to the spot where the cow had been
attacked. There they saw the lioness tearing away
at the carcase of the cow. They discussed the plan
of campaign, and decided that the best way to
approach their formidable foe was to advance in
single file. The boy in front was to carry the shield

for the lioness to jump upon when she made her leap, and as soon as she did this the second boy, who carried the assegai, was to stab the brute. These plucky youngsters carried out the programme to the letter.

The lioness, interrupted in her meal, looked up with a savage growl as the two picannins strode manfully towards her. With muzzle and paws red with blood she dropped to a crouching attitude and with a snarl of rage sprang upon the first boy, who manfully thrust the shield forward to receive the onslaught. Of course, he went down like a blade of grass and the lioness proceeded to worry and shake him as a terrier worries a rat; but in the meantime the other boy stabbed, and stabbed, and stabbed again until the lioness, mortally wounded, ceased from savaging her victim and, crawling away for a few yards, expired.

The boy who had borne the burden of the attack was terribly lacerated and bitten and eventually died. The other lad did not receive a single scratch. Strange to say, the male lion did not come to the assistance of his mate, but ran away and left the picannins in possession of the field.

CHAPTER XI

WE were not lucky in securing any elephants, so as we neared our own wagons we made up our minds to shoot some rhinoceros for the sake of the horn and the hide for sjambok.[1] They were extremely plentiful in this part, and we soon had a bag of 13. These we had skinned, and the hide cut up into strips, and sent for the wagon to fetch them. When it arrived we were enraged to find that a Bushman had taken one of our oxen. As this was the second that had been surreptitiously taken away by these slim little savages, I was determined to follow up the spoor and administer a salutary lesson.

Quickly getting on to the spoor I went in pursuit, and I had a pretty dance before I came up to the Bushman's kraal, for the thief had allowed for the possibility of pursuit, and had resorted to all sorts of tricks to mislead pursuers. To my disgust the kraal was deserted. I was not surprised, for these little forest people have no settled habitation. They gather a few sticks and a little grass where-

---

[1] Raw hide whips.

with to make a rude shelter and never remain in one spot for any length of time. In this case it was clear that they had not been gone long, and had evidently killed the ox and taken the meat in a half-dried condition with them. As, however, they were at least two days ahead of me, I did not consider it worth my while to follow up, and so returned to the wagons certainly in anything but a good humour, and vowing vengeance at some future date.

We rested for a few days, and then trekked to the east this time. This proved to be a much more profitable outing, for on the first day we picked up fresh elephant spoor. We slept upon it and made a fresh start in the morning, having been aroused several times during the night by the noise of elephants trumpeting.

We came upon the herd early in the morning, and I secured five bulls and Gifford three cows. Leaving the few boys we had with us to cut out the ivory, we retraced our steps towards the wagons, and on our way, only a mile from the wagons, came across a herd of buffalo. The opportunity was too good to be resisted, and I brought down three and Gifford one. We sent out as many boys as we could spare to skin and cut them, the hides being valuable for conversion into reims,[1] while the flesh was also most acceptable.

---

[1] A long thin strap made of raw hide.

As an instance of how lazy boys can be when there is no one to " boss them up," I may mention that the boys we had left to cut out the ivory were eight days before they put in an appearance. However, there was plenty of work to do preparing the buffalo skins for reims. Some of my readers may be interested in the process. The hide having been cut into strips the reims are hung to the branch of a suitable tree with a heavy weight tied to the bottom. A boy then takes a stick and twists the reim round and round as tightly as possible. Then he suddenly pulls the stick out, and the weight causes the reim to unwind with great speed. Just as it is on the point of stopping the stick is put in again, and the reim again wound up. This process is continued for three days, the reim being well greased in the meantime, and the result of this tedious process is a strip of hide as strong as wire rope and as soft and supple as a piece of velvet. From a bull buffalo about 50 reims can be cut, and from a cow about 40, worth in those days half-a-crown apiece.

I am not likely to forget this particular encounter with the buffalo, for I was chased by one, and she made me go for all I was worth. I make no secret of the fact that I turned and raced away from her as fast as poor old Dopper could go, for I think I would rather face a wounded lion than a buffalo. Dopper got me out of danger after a hard gallop, the result of his strenuous exertions being a swollen fetlock. Happily I was fortunate enough to have a bottle of embrocation with me, and with plenty of vigorous rubbing we were able to reduce the swelling.

I made up my mind to return to Shoshong, having ordered a lot of goods to arrive there. My intention was to start my brother trading there. I allowed Dopper to have a long rest, and I, using a horse that was no good for elephant shooting, shot other game for the sake of the skins and horns. A few giraffe, about a dozen eland, and 20 rhino fell to my gun, giving a big addition to an already large stock of reims, sjamboks and whips. Gifford went out one day and shot two very decent bull elephants, besides some rhino and an eland. It was five months since I left Shoshong, and in that time I had shot 53 elephants, yielding approximately 3,000 lbs. weight of ivory. During the same period Gifford had bagged 26.

During the fifteen days we were here preparing for our southern trek I had a great stroke of luck. Two fine cock ostriches came close to the wagons, and I managed to secure both. Their feathers were very fine, and each bird realised about £25. It was a great fluke for me, for I was a poor hand at shooting them. They are not at all easy prey, and I have been almost close up to them and then failed to bring them down. I remember on one occasion firing 16 shots with a small-bore gun at an ostrich, and in spite of that I did not get him. He was certainly hit, but he managed to get away, and I was quite unable to find him. I did not like leaving a wounded creature to die like that, but there was no help for it. I could not wait too long, for the nearest water was 15 miles back and 25 miles ahead, and though we had a little for ourselves, we were bound to get water for the sake of the oxen.

We reached Shoshong in good time, and I purchased a large quantity of goods from a Natal trader.

It was here that I parted with my faithful old hunting horse, "Dopper," for 900 lbs. weight of ivory. I was very sorry to part from him, for he had served me well, but he was getting the worse for wear, and, therefore, more or less unsafe when at close quarters with an elephant or buffalo.

I was offered two more horses, both guaranteed "salted." [1] I bought them, also a third one with a very good frame which I had seen standing with the horse sickness, and at that time had almost recovered. I took all chances, and gave poor little Johnny Stromboum £15 for him. It was a bargain

A horse which has had horse sickness and recovered. Afterwards immune from this disease.

for the horse got all right, and I shall have more to say about him later on.

There was no time to be lost if I wished to take advantage of the hunting season which lasts from May to November, when the trees are leafless, and there is less likelihood of losing sight of one's quarry.

At this stage I must introduce a well-known character. Those of my readers who have read Selous's first book will remember him mentioning a little Hottentot boy named Cigar, from Grahamstown. Well, I took Cigar with me on his first hunting trip in Matabeleland. It will, of course, be understood that Selous had not yet set foot in South Africa.

Cigar proved to be a good horseman as well as a fair shot.

I made a start about the middle of August, taking no fewer than five horses—four of my own and one belonging to the young Chief Khama which he lent me for the expedition. For the second time he himself came with me for a brief hunting trip, but on this occasion his little jaunt occupied only a few days as he only wanted to obtain some meat. We found giraffe at a well-known pan of water and shot eight, sufficient to fill the two wagons he had brought with him. I left him there as the process of drying the meat would occupy at least two or

three days. And at this spot I lost my first horse
through horse sickness. Perhaps it is needless to
add that it was one of the two that was sold to me
under a guarantee that it was " salted."

I had a big caravan on this trip: two wagons, a
double set of boys (forty-six mouths in all to feed)
and Cigar shooting on the halves system. Three
of the boys were to be paid wages and cash while
forty-two were each to receive for their services for
a three months' trip a musket with a supply of
powder, lead and caps. There is no doubt whatever
that I went in for " the grand " on this occasion and
for the first time launched out into extravagance.
I even included among my food supplies six tins of
jam, one pot of chow-chow, a cheese and, luxury of
luxuries, a case of small " Bass." What a contrast
to my earlier trips when dry biscuits and coffee for
breakfast, and ditto with a tin of sardines between
three of us for the big meal of the day!

We crossed the Macloutsie River and about five
miles further on, while I was resting in the wagon
trying to protect myself from the intense heat, my
driver galvanised me into life with the cry of " Elephant." There were at least thirty of them looking
at us! I didn't wait to saddle up. Seizing my gun
I caught the pony nearest to me, slipped the reim
into its mouth and galloped towards the herd. I

brought down three splendid bulls, their total yield of ivory being 300 lbs. Needless to say I celebrated my good luck by opening a bottle of the precious " Bass." It may interest some readers to know that the boys, in addition to cutting out the ivory, obtained a large quantity of fat. Elephant fat is very much like sheep-tail, is quite white, never gets hard, is excellent for cooking purposes and can be eaten on bread like butter.

Leaving the main road we continued down the Shasha, where I halted for the purpose of having a little novel form of sport. The idea is this: in the high river bank a cavern is scooped out leaving the smallest possible entrance and a small window or loophole. A pail of water is placed a few yards from the window and when the big animals come down to drink they offer an easy mark. Well, we constructed such a " fort " and leaving the wagons some three miles further down the river, I and a boy took up our positions. It is a most interesting experience to kneel at the window and watch the wonderful procession of animals of all sorts and sizes coming down to the river to drink. Of course one does not fire until the particular animal one is after comes into view. After kneeling at the porthole for some time my knees ached terribly and about midnight, to ease my bones, I sat down, though in this position I could see nothing.   As might have been expected I fell into a light doze and woke suddenly to find the cavern in complete darkness.   I wondered what had happened, for it was a bright moonlight night, and started fumbling about to find the " window."   Groping round the walls of the little cavern I at length felt the small opening, and then a deep " sniff " suddenly apprised me of the fact that some animal had thrust his nose in from the outside and was trying to " smell us out."   At this moment, however, it moved back allowing the moonlight to stream in and then I saw that my visitor was a magnificent male lion!   I was thankful that our front wall was very thick and was doubly grateful when he stalked majestically down the sand in the river bed and disappeared from view.   The temptation to fire was almost irresistible, but I was out for elephant, not lions, and my restraint was rewarded, for about four o'clock five bull elephants came down to drink and I got a nice young one carrying about 40 lbs. of ivory.

CHAPTER XII

CIGAR AND THE ELEPHANT—A UNICORN HORN—SIX ELE-
PHANTS WITH FIVE BULLETS—A NARROW ESCAPE—THE
BABY ELEPHANT AND ITS MOTHER—AN AMUSING SCENE
—A DISAPPOINTED BOER—BUSHMAN CATTLE THIEF AND
HIS DESERTS.

WE continued our journey down to the junction
of the Shasha and Simbokie to the spot where Napier
and I had previously seen the enormous herd of
elephant. We found elephants fairly plentiful and
had some profitable shooting. This is where Cigar
makes his first appearance as an elephant hunter.
I overheard him talking at the camp fire to the other
boys about the matter and from this it was quite
clear that though he was a famous hand with a gun
he did not altogether like the idea of getting too
close to an elephant. I was, therefore, not surprised to find that when it came to an actual encounter he was not a success. He fired a number
of shots but did not get anything, then he lost the
elephants and once or twice got lost himself and had
to sleep out in the bush. During the whole time he
was with me he never shot an elephant, and eventually I put him on to shoot rhinoceros, sending him
in a direction directly opposite to the one we took,

on account of the noise he made with continuous firing.

He mentioned one day that he had fired at and wounded a rhino with an exceptionally long horn, but the animal had got away. Curious to know whether he was " drawing the long bow " I went out in that direction and, directed by a number of vultures sitting in the trees, I soon located the carcase. It certainly had a very pretty horn, 3 ft. $10\frac{1}{2}$ ins. in length and with a very small butt. In fact it was so unlike the usual rhino horn that I afterwards showed it to a man as a fine specimen of a unicorn horn.

I was away from the wagons a whole week, having shot eight elephants meanwhile. There was a nice shower of rain the night I returned to camp and in the morning the boys told me they had heard elephants down the river. I made it a rule never to hunt on Sundays, but it was such a beautiful morning after the rain that I could not resist a ride out, if only to see which way they had gone. Their fresh spoor was visible less than a mile from the wagons, and before I anticipated anything of the kind the herd was right in front of me.

Upon examining my pouch I found I had only four bullets there, with one in the gun. However, I set to work with my five bullets. With the first

I secured a cow, the bulls being too far away. Following up the herd I got a bull with a lucky shot, shooting him at a distance of 12 feet, without even putting the gun to my shoulder. This was not my usual practice, but in this case he was lying in wait for me and it was not until I was almost on top of him that I and my horse saw him. The horse swerved and I pulled the trigger simultaneously. When at last I was able to pull him up, my hands were very much knocked about for I had been galloping along holding on to the weapon by the muzzle and that, with a runaway horse, was decidedly awkward and painful. Upon going back to the elephant I found that my chance shot had, fortunately for me, proved fatal and he was lying down close to where I shot him. Upon looking him over I noticed a curious little knob on the shoulder and pulling out my knife, I cut a slit in the hide and there I found my bullet as perfect as when it was moulded. Firing at such close quarters it had passed through the elephant and nearly out the other side. This bullet came in very useful for with it I got another elephant. In fact, every one of my shots that day were effective, so that with five bullets I performed the unique feat of getting six elephants. I might have had many more if I had had a further supply of bullets. The herd subsequently ran close to the wagons and the boys certainly ought to have had one, at least. One of them did make an attempt with Cigar's gun and for a time they appeared to have had some excitement. The dogs had tackled one elephant and kept him at bay, and it was their noise that induced the boy to run out with Cigar's gun and take a shot. Unfortunately he was not a good marksman and as his first shot failed to bring his quarry down he had to run back to the wagon for more ammunition. When he returned the elephant had bolted and though the boy followed up the spoor he was not able to find the wounded animal.

I must tell here of a curious incident I saw, early in the morning, before I started the herd on the run. Creeping closely up to the herd I saw a young elephant digging vigorously at the root of a mimosa tree, of which elephants are very fond. He would loosen the ground with his tusks, scrape away the earth with his foot, feel the root with his trunk and give it a pull and if it was still firm would use his tusk and foot again.

An old cow, his mother, was standing alongside, apparently asleep, at any rate taking no notice of her industrious offspring, but when at last the baby elephant, by dint of much hard work, snapped the succulent root and was about to put it into his mouth, the old cow promptly reached out with her trunk and calmly took it away.

The baby elephant screamed with impotent rage and rushed at its mother trying to recover the root. The old lady, however, merely kept turning her tail towards him, put the root into her mouth and munched away, entirely unmoved by the almost human cries of her lusty child. It was a most amusing performance and I sat and watched them for quite a long time.

I left the wagons again and during the week got on the spoor of three bulls. I came up with them only a short distance away and had just got the third down when a man came galloping up at top speed. He proved to be a Boer, Piet Jacobs, the father of the man to whom I had sold old Dopper. He said he had been on the spoor of these elephants since dawn, and had come some fifteen miles after them. He was greatly disappointed, so to console him I promised him some meal, lead, and tin for hardening his bullets. He said he would come down to my wagons on the following week. When he put in an appearance I was somewhat surprised to find that he had brought his wagon with him, for I had not asked him to join forces with me and preferred hunting alone.

However, we went out together during the week

and came across a herd of elephants. These the old chap disturbed by firing at and killing a fat zebra, just as we were about to get to work. The old man's excuse was that he wanted meat and that zebra flesh was most delicious. It may have been so to him, but I could not touch it. However, we camped for the night, the zebra was cut up, and between old Piet and the boys, there was nothing left in the morning, save the skin and bones.

Next day we did better, though our bag only consisted of cows with about 20 lbs. of ivory each. I got five and Piet six. Next morning we came up to an old bull with a magnificent pair of tusks. We agreed to syndicate him and shoot him jointly. This we did, our two bullets quickly bringing him to earth, and so good were the tusks that I gave the old man £10 for his, so as to keep the pair intact.

When I told him that I was going to shift camp that day and going down the river, he replied, as I hoped and expected, that he would not come. He said he was frightened of getting into the fly.

I crossed over the Shashani river and found the elephants plentiful, five bulls and two cows being my first day's bag.

My old boy, the driver, subsequently told me that the herd came right across the front of the wagons. He stood and watched them go past and then let the dogs go. They promptly tackled and turned out of the herd a very large bull.

"Why didn't you shoot him?" I asked. "You had a gun."

"Yes, baas," he replied, "I had a gun but he looked too big for me; and another thing, baas, I cannot run!"

I asked Cigar why he did not shoot and he replied that he did not like to shoot elephant when on foot in case he might be charged by the wounded animal.

Seeing that we were well into the heart of the elephant country I gave instructions to build a kraal round the wagons and got nicely settled so that everything would be safe from the lions at nights. This we did and also put up a shed for the horses.

Our precautions against midnight visitors were taken none too soon. In fact not soon enough, for on the forthcoming morning before it was quite finished, the ox herd came to me and reported that an ox was missing, and that he had his suspicion that a two-legged lion had spirited it away. I had suffered quite enough from the thieving propensities of the Bushmen and was determined that on this occasion someone would meet trouble.

Throwing out a number of boys to get the spoor, we quickly picked up the direction the ox had been

driven and started on the trail early in the morning.
Those who knew the ways of oxen will hardly think
it possible that one beast could be driven, especially
at night, but there was no mistaking it this time
and it just shows what a wild man of the woods can
do.   The spoor lay straight ahead and as I had
good spoorers with me and calculated that as we
were not more than two hours behind him at the
start we should soon come up with the thief.

We had gone some distance when we saw drops
of blood and I also saw that the ox was walking
lame.   This spurred us to increased speed and about
three o'clock in the afternoon we saw the ox about a
mile ahead of us.   Pulling my horse together, I
galloped forward and saw that behind the ox, driving it for all it was worth, was a Bushman—carrying
a gun.

He soon heard the sound of my horse's hoofs
and turning round promptly put the gun to his
shoulder and fired at not more than 100 yards distance.   It was a narrow shave for the bullet struck
right in front of the horse, sending a cloud of dust
all over me.   Then the Bushman commenced to run,
but he did not go very far——

I drove the ox back to the boys.   The poor brute
was very lame, for the Bushman, with fiendish ingenuity, had chopped it in the hock with an axe so

that it could not outrun him. Of course, it was useless for transport purposes, so I killed it and told
the boys to carry as much meat as they could to
the wagons and to hang the remainder in the trees.

They were very curious to know what had become of the Bushman. I told them he had run
away—and so he had.

CHAPTER XIII

BUFFALO DANGERS—A SAVAGE ASSAULT—A WAGON ACCI-
DENT—AMONG THE LIONS—MY HORSE KILLED—A DAY
OF SLAUGHTER.

AFTER cutting up the recaptured oxen we had a
long journey back to the wagons and did not arrive
till after nightfall. A grilled steak and a long
night's sleep, however, soon made amends. I woke
next morning to find that the other quarantined
horse was sick and by ten o'clock he was dead, so
rapid is the operation of horse sickness. Next day
I was among the elephants again, shot eight cows,
averaging about 24 lbs. weight of ivory each, whilst
I also secured a couple of bulls, each yielding 90
lbs. of ivory. Several rhinoceros also fell to my
gun, giving me plenty of sjambok and rhino horn.

While on the trip, I saw a magnificent herd of
buffalo. There were many hundreds of them and
they offered a tempting opportunity which I did
not refuse. I, however, only brought down two,
for the sake of their skins and meat. Personally
I was never very keen on shooting buffalo, for the
exciting sport offered too much risk, both to one's
self and to one's horse, and while hunting in the bush
it is not wise to expose a valuable horse to unneces-

sary danger. In my opinion, the buffalo is more dangerous than any other animal in South Africa, and tackling a herd of them is the most risky sport in the world. With these phenomenally cunning animals one never knows where safety lies, and just when you imagine you are following up a stampeded herd you find yourself charged by one of them from the side or rear. I would never return on the track taken by buffalo for fear that a wounded one would be waylaying me. The trouble is that they are so unnaturally cute in their manœuvre. They will hide the whole of their body in a thick bush and when the unsuspecting hunter comes along there is not much chance of mistake.

Many people have been killed by the angry beasts. I saw one very narrow escape. A young man named Blanch had borrowed a horse, valued at £75, from a Mr. Hudson, and we were going towards the Tati to return the animal to its owner. I was in front and I and Blanch had only gone a short distance when a couple of grunts caused me to look round and I saw Blanch sprawled on the ground and the hind-quarters of his horse in the air. Behind them was a wicked-looking buffalo that had made a most effective charge from the rear. Without waiting a second, I brought my gun up and firing from the saddle, put a bullet into the buffalo's shoulder.   He gave two turns and fell down dead.

Poor Blanch was in a terrible state, not so much about himself as about the borrowed horse, for the buffalo had ripped its stomach completely open with its horns, inflicting a mortal wound.   In fact he was dead within the hour and as Blanch was not in a financial position to pay for him, the loss fell upon Mr. Hudson, the owner.

Next to the buffalo I should place the South African " tiger " [1] as the most dangerous animal in the country.   He is spotted like the leopard but, whereas the leopard has a black spot within a yellow centre and has a mane, the tiger has a black spot with a yellow centre.   The " tiger's " quickness and ferocity are remarkable.   I once saw one of them kill three dogs in one leap.

When we crossed the Tati and arrived at Hudson's place, he was naturally very much distressed at the loss of his horse.   I sold him one of mine for £40—a quite good salted riding horse but useless for elephant shooting.   I had now only three horses left, two of whom had done a great deal of work, while the third, the one I bought from Stromboum, was in prime condition and ready for my next outing.   The fates ordained, however, that I should never ride him.

---

[1] In South Africa a leopard is called a tiger.   A cheta is called a leopard.

His tragic end came in this wise: I had told my boy on a certain day to shift the wagons to another water, about seven miles from the Shasshani while I went out with my gun. Later on in the day, upon arriving at the place where the wagons ought to have been, I found to my surprise that they had not put in an appearance. Suspecting something wrong, I rode out to a rise some distance from the river bank and saw the wagons in a valley some distance away. I rode down to them and found that they had had an accident, having broken the main bolt of the wagon coming through a small rivulet, but they had repaired the damage and were now ready to move on. Looking round I said, " Where are the horses? "

The old boy replied that they were there a few moments ago and that he had sent a boy to bring them along. I did not at all like the idea of their being out of sight, so immediately called up some boys, picked up the spoor and by 11 o'clock had tracked the horses back to where they had camped the previous night. At this spot I came up with the boy who had been sent out for them. He was crawling along at a snail's pace quite unconcernedly. Telling him to follow on as rapidly as possible I hurried forward and just as I had reached the spot where the wagons had been standing, one of the horses came running back towards me in a state of abject terror and very excited.

I promptly caught him, put the reim in his mouth, handed him to one of the boys and hurried forward. I had only gone a short distance further on when I saw by the spoor that the horses had started galloping. A short distance further ahead I saw a lion spoor by the side of that of the horses, and from the way the spoor showed its impress on the sand I could tell that he was bounding along at top speed.

Two hundred yards further on I came to my beautiful horse lying dead. Jumping to the ground and examining the spoor I could see that two lions had made the attack and had apparently left their prey because of my arrival. A minute or two later one of them stood up in front of me about 50 yards away.

I fired and dropped him on his own spoor, and without waiting a second loaded again and walked up slowly towards him. As I did so another one rose close by, and taking rapid aim I also finished his account. Then we retraced our steps, and had not gone far when we saw a lioness, evidently of the same troop. Carefully working my way round I fired and broke her neck. I felt a little better after revenging myself for the loss of my horse, though still very upset by the occurrence.

Before reaching the wagon we saw that elephants had crossed our spoor since we passed along an hour or so before, and I immediately determined to follow it up. We had been on it for about four miles when we heard a noise and stopped to listen. After a few minutes we heard it again and it sounded like the rumble of an elephant's stomach. Both the boys agreed with me that it was an elephant and I promptly got ready for work by emptying a pound of powder into my pocket, and proceeding cautiously in the direction of the sound.

All at once I saw something like a large blue rock, but one of the boys was sharper than I and claimed it as his game. Upon getting close we found it to be a dead rhino I had wounded some days previously. But tearing at the carcase was a big lion, and it was his growlings we had heard!

Now, of course, the valiant boy who had claimed the " game " wanted to hang back and showed symptoms of running away, so I jumped off my horse, seized the boy by the ear, and marched him towards the lion and the rhino, telling him that as he claimed it as his game he must go and take possession of it. He certainly did not like the idea. His jaw shook with fear, his eyes were starting out of his head, while his face went the colour of dirty ashes. However, I dragged him along, and as the ground was quite open save for one bush the boy had every reason to fear that I meant to offer him up as a sacrifice. He hung back as much as he could but was too frightened to howl.

By this time, when we were only a few yards away, the lion had detected our presence, or at any rate had heard something. He stopped his meal, commenced to gaze steadily around him, but as he did so I fired. The lion gave a spring, and as he did so the boy did the same, but they raced off in totally different directions.

I had made no mistake with my shot. The bullet tore the lungs to pieces; he gave one loud groan and expired.

I was still standing at this bush, re-loading, when to my astonishment another lion made his appearance. He had evidently been inside the rhino, gorging himself to his heart's content in the soft interior. He was smothered with filth, blood and grease. I promptly fired and hit him. He seemed very surprised, made two huge leaps into the air with the blood gushing from his mouth and nostrils, and then rolled over, dead.

My boy did not attempt to cut the rhino's horn off and relinquished all claim to the prize.

As it was getting late and I had no blankets and no food, I decided to make as quickly as possible for the nearest water in order to make a camp for the night, it being far too dangerous to attempt to reach the wagons. Arriving at a pool of water we off-saddled. I told the boys off to cut grass for the horses and some to gather sufficient wood to keep fires going throughout the night.

It was already sundown, so I told them to hurry up. A few minutes later the boys who were gathering wood shouted: "Lions! Lions!" Telling a boy to catch the horses I ran towards the boys who had given the alarm, and they pointed to a spot where they said the lions had gone. Running forward I came upon the boy who was cutting grass. He said he was in a little dip busily cutting when he heard a slight rustle, saw a shadow, and looking up saw that two lions had leaped right over him to the opposite ridge.

Taking the direction he pointed out, the boy following, I saw one of the pair, the male, about 70 yards away. I fired and dropped him with one shot.

And then I did a silly thing. Forgetting my usual precaution of always reloading after firing a shot, I walked forward, followed by the boy. We were not four yards away when the lion suddenly lifted up his mighty head, opened wide his mouth and showed four beautiful fangs.

The boy and myself made a simultaneous leap,

and it would be hard to say who won that sprint race! Presently I recovered from fright to look round, but seeing nothing following I halted. Having reloaded my gun, I returned very cautiously, but the lion was quite dead and had not, apparently, moved from its original position.

The boy who had returned with me suddenly grew alert and said he could hear the lioness calling for its mate. We waited silently and then he drew my attention to a dim object about 100 yards away. I could not aim very accurately on account of the twilight, but I drew the trigger on the best aim I could take and from the roaring that ensued it was obvious that I had wounded her. We went nearer and found that I had broken her backbone.

Before leaving I cut a fat piece of meat off the old male's ribs. It was something to eat at any rate, and was not at all of bad flavour, though very tough.

We went out the next morning to have a look at the lioness whom we had left struggling in the darkness. She was now quite dead and stiff.

This was the most eventful day of my life with the lions. I should not have bothered with them now had it not not been that they started by killing my horse and I wanted a little revenge.

In those days the skins were valueless and we never dreamed of skinning lions.

CHAPTER XIV

END OF THE TRIP—RECORD ELEPHANT "BAG"—AN UN-
CONVENTIONAL SMOKER—A YEAR'S IVORY; 5,000 LBS.—
ADVENTURES WITH THE ELEPHANTS—A CASK OF PEACH
BRANDY—AND HOW IT WAS TAPPED

UPON reaching the wagons, which were about six miles down the river, I had to rest a little while, for the horses were footsore, and it was necessary to shoe them. As I had a few old shoes by me, together with nails, I set to work as an amateur farrier and carried out the job more or less creditably.

As my time was drawing short I determined to get away on another trip as quickly as possible, so, taking nearly all the boys, whom I loaded with sufficient grain to last the horses ten days, we set out. On the second day we came up with the elephant and five bulls and five cows fell to my gun in one day. This was my " record," for neither before nor since did I equal that bag. It was a double—record for one day, and a record from one herd. We cut out the ivory and buried it, pushed off again, and once more came up with a good herd, and then having secured four nice bulls averaging about 90 lbs. of ivory each, I returned to the wagons on horseback, telling the boys to follow on. It was

143

several days before they put in an appearance, and
what a leg-weary crowd they were.

But when the next day I told them that we
were about to return to Shoshong their weariness
was forgotten. They danced and shouted for joy,
and immediately began to prepare for the return
journey on the morrow. It was simply amazing to
see the amount and variety of rubbish they had
accumulated. They were just as bad as magpies
for gathering all the worthless rubbish round them,
and when I saw what it amounted to, I had to put
my foot down and forbid the carrying of much of
the stuff on the wagons on account of the weight.

The wagons were already fully loaded. One
was loaded with reims, whips and sjamboks, while
on the other was the ivory—about 3,000 lbs. in
weight.

Early in November I left the Sashani and made
for the main road, passing the Tati. Coming to
the hills between the Ramaquabane and the Tati I
came upon fresh elephant spoor and, following it a
short distance, soon came up with a fine herd and
brought down eight tuskers. On this occasion I
had some white spectators, for I had come upon the
camp formed by a party brought up by Sir John
Swinburne, and they turned out to watch the elephant hunt.

These good people were not hunting, but gold mining. They had built themselves a nice house and were doing themselves quite well. I camped with them that night and we celebrated the occasion with a very jovial sing-song. We kept it going till the small hours, for they were not at all particular about bed, while as for me it was not such a common experience to have a jolly lot of white men as companions that I was in a hurry to miss any of the good fellowship. By the time the concert was over it did not take anybody long to go to sleep.

I stayed with them some few days, during which period I shot them a fine fat giraffe for meat, and then proceeded on my journey. I reached Shoshong towards the end of November, very well pleased with myself. During this one year I had secured one hundred and eleven elephants, the ivory weighing about 5,000 lbs.—not a bad year's result.

I remained in Shoshong about four months, while my brother went on a trading expedition into the Transvaal with a lot of soft goods.[1] As it turned out, these goods were of no use for the trade there, and my brother, instead of making money, sustained a loss of about £200. He went in for buying and trading cattle. Then he got lung-sickness

---

[1] Soft goods, dry goods.

among them, had them inoculated, and as it was in wet weather he lost more than half of them! When he returned with his tale of woe he also brought with him a fifteen-gallon cask of peach brandy (of which more, later on).

The hunters from the Zambesi and Lake Ngami did not put in an appearance till December and January, but upon their arrival I secured a very fine lot of ivory and ostrich feathers, for cash and barter, to say nothing of my portion of the " bag " for the goods, food, etc., I had supplied them on credit when they went up. Among the crowd at this time were several new hands who had come up from Grahamstown and Natal to " chance their arm." Mention of them reminds me of a little incident that happened on one of my earlier trips. There were a lot of us together in the MaKobbies mountains, the first hills south of the Mangwe River (where a number of Barotses lived until old Mzili- katse wiped most of them out in 1863).

Our party consisted of Chapman, Francis, Phillips, Gifford, Leask (of Klerksdorp), myself, an old Griqua (Haans High) and three of his fol- lowers, all on horseback. We struck the spoor of three bull elephants, followed them for nearly the whole of the day and then Chapman rushed ahead and fired. I saw no other elephant at the time, but seeing the old Griqua racing ahead with his boys, I followed, saw two elephants, told the Griqua which one he might take and soon brought mine to a standstill, while Leask, Phillips and Gifford put in the finishing touches. He proved to have the heaviest ivory of the three, viz., over 100 lbs., while Chapman's went 80 lbs. and the old Griqua's 70 lbs.

I have never heard a man describe so humorously a whirlwind chase after elephants as did Phillips in recounting my proceedings that day. I had followed the elephant across some old Kafir cultivated lands, where the natives had followed the usual practice of cutting off the trees about four feet from the ground, piling the branches round the stump, and burning it off when dry. This practice left the place littered with half-burned and rotten branches and my powerful horse seemed to the others like unto an animated threshing machine as it tore across the land and threw up a continuous mass of twigs and branches with its hind feet, scattering all my companions and compelling them to keep a respectable distance in the rear.

But to resume. I sold all my produce at Shoshong and realised a considerable sum of money, and in April returned to my old hunting ground, above the Tuli River.

I had a real " greenhorn " with me, a youngster named Hillier who had run away from his uncle in Cape Town. The uncle was the captain of a small schooner and the lad had been apprenticed to him to learn sailoring. But sailoring was not to his liking, so he gave his uncle the slip, got up to Grahamstown and thence to the Transvaal where he made the acquaintance of my brother, who brought him along with him to Shoshong. It was his ambition to see elephants in their wild state, and as he had a beautiful and speedy horse that he had ridden all the way up from Grahamstown, there was no reason why his desire should not be gratified.

I learned to sigh over that horse. He was all right for shooting ordinary game, but with elephant he was a rotter. He would get excited, refuse to stand still to enable one to get a shot from his back, while if one got off he would keep running round one. I very nearly shot him once or twice as he tried this circus performance with me.

We had been on the Shashani about a month when the brothers Jennings, accompanied by Blanch, appeared on the scene. While we were having breakfast next morning the boys shouted to us that they heard elephants trumpeting, and it did not take us long to saddle up and be off.

Young Hillier was greatly excited and eager. He selected a gun I used for shooting small game and was quickly in the saddle and off on his speedy mount. He meant to be there all right, but alas for the good resolutions of youth! In the first five hundred yards, just as he was nearing an elephant, his horse fell over a fallen tree, and Hillier came a fearful cropper. He was a plucky one, however, for he was quickly on his feet and fired both barrels at the elephant, but so far as I could see with no result. However, I had no time to wait. I was soon at work on my own account, and brought down four bulls and three cows. Jennings got a cow with one tusk and Blanch had drawn a blank.

When I got back to camp I found that Hillier had burst my gun. It appeared that when he was thrown the muzzle of the gun became choked with sand, and when he fired both barrels split. I took four inches off but it was never the same weapon again.

To celebrate our first day's hunting I announced that I would give the party a jollification in the shape of some peach brandy. The before-mentioned cask, brought up from the Transvaal by my brother, was accordingly produced, and I was carefully drawing off a large dish full of the delectable spirit when out popped a reed. I did not take much notice of it, but when I saw a second I grew suspicious, and upon examining it and finding it quite fresh my first fears were confirmed. The cask had been tapped; but by whom? I looked at old Haans but he smiled an inscrutable smile and shook his hoary head. When I demanded information he referred me to the other boy, Farrel, who upon being taxed, had to admit that he certainly had enjoyed a little sip or two through a reed.

A sip or two! When we came to taste it it was weak brandy and water! Whether my brother had been nicely " sold " in the Transvaal and had bought one gallon of brandy and fourteen gallons of water at the price of pure brandy I cannot say, but I have a shrewd suspicion that the Griquas knew more than they cared to admit, and we strongly suspected them of drawing off most of the contents with glorious generosity (to themselves!) and filling up the cask with water.

Anyway, the peach brandy, that was to have been such a luxury, comfort and consoler on the trip, was a failure. Well, no, not quite, for Jennings and Blanch, who were both deeply grieved over the fraud, found even in the watered contents a source of considerable attraction during the two days they remained. Apart from the loss in value I was not greatly concerned for I did not drink spirits in those days. It would, however, have been useful in many ways.

After two days Jennings and Blanch returned to their wagons, which were standing high up on the Simbookie River, where I afterwards joined them and took part in a trip after elephant which brought three young bulls and three cows to my bag.

CHAPTER XV

TWO HAPPY-GO-LUCKY HUNTERS—HOW THEY FRIGHTENED
THE ELEPHANTS—GIRAFFE FOR THE POT—A STARTLING
EXPERIENCE—"WATER, WATER, GIVE US WATER"—DAN
FRANCIS' MINING PARTY—QUARREL WITH KHAMA'S
NATIVES

ON my way out I ran up against a number of
hunters and others coming down from the Zambesi
district. They were travelling by the Tati. I did
a little trade with them, securing a fair amount of
ivory in return. At a place called Gowkwe—where
it will be remembered I had hung the koodoo meat
in a tree—I met Mr. Hume and Sir Percy Douglas's son, who were out on a shooting trip. Nothing
would do but they must make me go back with them
for a few days in order that they might get an
elephant.

After some demur I agreed to go back for a fortnight, only on condition that they would hold out
for that length of time in the elephant country.
They at once agreed. As I told them it was useless taking our wagons for such a short time, we
decided to leave the heavy gear behind. Leaving
my wagons at the Gowkwe, just below the old Tati
drift, we all mounted our horses and turned our
faces to the northward. I explained to Hume and

Sir Percy Douglas's son, that if they wanted elephant they must on no account shoot anything else, otherwise the sound of their weapons would frighten all the elephants away long before they could be seen by the hunters.

They listened to all I had to say, but shortly after we crossed the Tati and had surmounted a high ridge, a little black rhinoceros crossed our path. The two sportsmen immediately forgot their resolution. They put their new breech-loaders to their shoulders, and to me it sounded like a regiment of soldiers at work.

I promptly lost a little bit of my temper. I reminded them of what I had told them about not shooting anything but elephants and told them, without any circumlocution, that by their stupid and unnecessary fusillade they had spoiled the shooting for the day and it was now only eight o'clock in the morning. I pointed out that by this time there would be no elephants within seven or eight miles of us, for every animal within that radius would have taken fright.

However, we went on a little further when we came upon a very fine lot of giraffe. Hume could not resist the opportunity and begged me to let him have " just one." As I knew the elephant were hopeless for the day I said, " all right," and we cautiously moved towards the giraffe which were about a mile and a half away. On our way, I showed my companions what they had missed by their noisy assault upon the rhino, by pointing out to them, right across our path, the fresh spoor of seven bull elephants—evidently started off on the run by the reports of the guns. My companions looked a bit sick over it, but they were not long down-hearted and their spirits quickly recovered at a nearer view of the giraffe. The herd was contentedly browsing on the tender buds and young leaves of the trees which were just beginning to sprout.

As a supply of giraffe meat was likely to prove a welcome addition to my larder, I went away on the right, while my two companions went straight ahead. I bowled over a fat cow and they shot two or three. They were highly delighted with themselves and could not have been much better pleased if they shot two or three bull elephants. They faithfully promised that next day they would not shoot for meat but would withhold their fire till elephant were in sight.

The boys skinned and cut up the giraffe and after enjoying juicy, grilled steaks, we had the remainder of the meat hung in the trees and protected with branches from the ravages of the birds.

Next day, at day-break, we set off after elephant, but though we kept as silent as could be there was not the spoor of a single elephant to be seen. The previous day's fusillade had driven them out of the district. Seeing that elephants were hopeless, I told them they had better amuse themselves with shooting what they liked and we would slowly make our way back to the wagons.

They enjoyed themselves after their own fashion and were quite contented with their sport. We arrived at the outspan four days after our departure and my companions immediately started on their ·return southwards. I also got away with my wagons and went on from there to Serula. That morning I had brought a giraffe right alongside the road within 100 yards of the wagons, shooting it there, when I was startled at seeing a number of white men come stumbling forward with pannikins in their hands shouting: "Water, water, give us water!" and holding out their pannikins in a despairing way. There was little doubt that they were in a bad way and had been suffering severely from thirst. In fact they were in such a condition that it would have been positively dangerous for them to drink the muddy stuff in the water-hole near our wagons.

I therefore told them that if they would wait

a few minutes I would soon give them something to quench their thirst. I quickly prepared a big kettle of tea for them and as its heat prevented them from " swilling " large quantities, their thirst agonies were relieved without danger to themselves. I gave them a couple of pannikins each. As they regaled themselves, impatiently waiting for the tea to cool, others of their party came straggling in, in a state of exhaustion. I kept the kettle on the boil so as to be ready for them. They were a big party, 29 altogether, and they taxed my tea-making resources to the utmost.

Presently their wagons turned up in charge of Mr. Dan Francis (who paid a passing visit to Bulawayo only a few weeks ago). I warned them all not to touch the dirty water at the water-hole unless it was boiled, unless they were anxious to get typhoid fever, and offered them such water as I had in hand.

We remained there all next day, while the party rested. They were a curious lot of men, all of them miners, who were being taken up to what are now the Tati Concessions Mines.

And they were a hungry lot too. In one day they finished two sides of the big giraffe I had shot.

On the following morning Dan Francis put them on to clean out one of the dirty water-pits in order to obtain a supply of fresh water. While they were engaged in this work, I heard a terrible squabble in progress and soon there was something like a free fight between the miners and some of Khama's natives.

Francis and I ran over and it was lucky we did, for matters had assumed a serious stage. I told Francis to tell the men to put down their shovels, which they were about to use as weapons, warning him that if the white men made an attack and killed one of the natives, there would be a heap of trouble all around.

Upon enquiring into the trouble I found it was caused by the discovery in the water-hole of a pair of gemsbok's horns. These are, of course, very long and straight, with sharp points, and the natives had " planted " these in the mud of the water hole so that cattle or wild beasts coming down to drink would be probed by the horns. The white men having found the horns in the hole claimed them, while the natives who had seen the horns recovered were equally vehement in their assertion that the horns belonged to them—which unquestionably was the case, though the white men did not understand or did not appreciate their point of view, and refused to give them up.

However, I was able to induce Francis to get the horns delivered up to there rightful owners. After this we parted on excellent terms of good fellowship. They went north and I went south.

Thus ended my trip of 1869. I went in again in the following year but met with no special adventure.

CHAPTER XVI

AN IMPUDENT THEFT—A HEADMAN'S HAUL—MORE CAT-
TLE THEFTS—AND SWIFT PUNISHMENT—ADVENTURES
WITH LIONS—AN UNPLEASANT CORNER—BETWEEN
GRASS FIRE AND A WOUNDED LION

IT was at this spot I was made the victim of a
most impudent theft. I mentioned in a previous
chapter that when I left Shoshong I had very little
grain, as owing to a very bad harvest the natives
had very little, and such as they had they wanted
for themselves and did not care to sell. The quantity I had brought in with me was by this time nearly
exhausted, and it was necessary that I should secure
some food for my boys.

Upon returning to the wagons after my short
spell with Jennings and Blanch, I made preparations to purchase some grain from the natives. Taking out the hind axle and wheels of the wagon I
made a body to it, composed of raw-hides. It was
a good, serviceable vehicle for the conveyance of
grain, even if it was not particularly artistic, and
was large enough to carry twelve bags comfortably.
In this improvised cart I packed from £80 to £100
worth of trading goods, in the shape of half a dozen
muskets, ten bags of powder, some lead and caps,

a quantity of beads, blankets, hats, jackets and shirts, also some brass wire and Kafir picks. I placed it all in the charge of my old boy, Hans, with instructions what to do in the matter of barter and exchange.

He was absent about 12 days and then returned absolutely empty-handed, with all the trade goods gone and not a bag of mealies in their place. For the moment I was almost too furious to speak, but I soon saw that something was amiss for poor Hans was obviously in a state of great distress and nearly starved to death.

I was not long in gleaning the full particulars. It appeared that when he set off on his trading expedition he arrived at a certain kraal in the hills late in the afternoon. He slept there that night, and in the morning went to see the head-man, who listened to his story and condescendingly told him he could bring his goods up to the kraal and he would inspect them. Hans, having stated that he was willing to trade cattle, sheep and grain, went back to his camp, brought up the cart and off-loaded all the things on to some blankets for the inspection of the lordly head-man, who surveyed the articles with a critical air, and was kind enough to say that they met with his approval.

He then told his men to take charge of the

goods and place them in the huts. Hans stood by, but just when he expected the head-man to produce the necessary cattle, grain, etc., in exchange, the old villain told him to inspan and clear out or he would quickly blot him out!

Old Hans needed no second threat, for he knew the character of this head-man too well to doubt that the threat was genuine and that he was lucky even to receive warning. Without even waiting to get a bit of food he came back a good deal faster than he went!

I found out from some of my boys that this head-man M'Tibi was a notorious scoundrel. He was afterwards prominent for his cruelties during the subsequent Matabele Rebellion. For the moment, however, I allowed his theft to pass unnoticed. I could not afford 12 to 14 days to go up and recover my goods, but, registering a silent vow of vengeance, I treasured up his impudence and made up my mind to get my own back during my next trip. Which I did, with interest, as will be manifest at a later stage.

We worked our way quietly up the river and I went out shooting alone. I had got fresh elephant spoor some seven or eight miles from the wagons but did not feel inclined to follow it up for they were only a paltry lot of cows. Just at this juncture, about 11 A.M., I fell in with three Boers, one Smidt, and his two sons.   They were on the spoor of one of their oxen that had been taken or had strayed from their wagons, and I joined them.   Within a very short distance we found there was a second ox. I did not know whose it was, but it afterwards transpired—what I did not then suspect—that one of my own oxen had also been taken during the night.

I asked Smidt what he was going to do and he replied grimly:

" Follow it up and fire into the niggers."

" I'm with you," I replied, " for I also have had enough of their thievish propensities. *But send your niggers back!*"   This they did and told them to go back to their wagons, which were on the Shasha, about seven miles from my wagons and nearly opposite those of Jennings.   I also sent my boys back.

We four white men followed the trail till dark, and though the spoor was getting quite fresh we were compelled to relinquish any further pursuit until morning, owing to our inability to see.

We made a camp for the night and as we sat round the fire we could hear, a considerable distance off, the sound of revelry.   We knew then we were not far behind the cattle thieves who, not suspecting pursuit, were indulging in a wild orgie to celebrate their successful raid upon the cattle of the white men. Their shouting and dancing continued far into the night and we snatched a few hours' sleep, by no means placated by their jubilations which, we knew, betokened that one of the oxen had been killed and partly eaten.

At daybreak we resumed our pursuit and creeping cautiously through the bush we came up to the thieves' kraal just as the dawn was breaking. To my amazement I saw one of my oxen standing there —the quietest and laziest beast I possessed. The Dutchmen's had been killed to provide for the feast, and the unconsumed portions were still on the ground. There was not much of it left for they had gorged themselves the whole night through and those who know the Bushman, or any native for that matter, know how much meat he can pack into his anatomy when he has the opportunity. There were three men, two women, and two or three little children, and they had evidently gorged themselves to repletion.

It was the men's last feast, however. I had no quarrel with the women and children, but we had been too often robbed by the wicked little Bushmen to have much sympathy for them.

I recovered my ox and drove him back to the

wagons, Smidt and his sons continuing their journey to their own camp. Working my way along the Shasha I got elephants once or twice and arrived eventually at the old road above Ramaquabane Drift. Telling the boys to erect a strong kraal, I went out on horseback after elephant and succeeded in getting three. After a bath in the river and supper, I turned into bed but about eleven o'clock we heard the roaring of a lion, though as it appeared to be a long way off we did not take much notice of it.

Presently, however, the lions drew near to our kraal. So near in fact that the oxen started to stampede. The first thing I realised was that old Blessman, the one that had been stolen by the Bushmen, was just coming through the fence. As he was the laziest of the span and always the last to move, I naturally assumed that he would be the last to leave the kraal, so without waiting to dress I sprang up barefoot, clad only in a shirt, and made a rush to turn the line of bullocks back to the kraal.

Only a few seconds elapsed before a tremendous roar, a cloud of dust, and the bellow of a bullock, told me that the lion was already at work. I fired at the spot where the commotion occurred, with what result I could not say.

The same morning at daybreak I was up and,

accompanied by two or three boys, followed up the cattle tracks, and came up with the frightened animals towards the Tati. They had certainly been badly scared, but we soon tamed them down. Upon counting them I found that one was missing, and upon returning to camp about 3 o'clock old Hans said one had been killed on the road not 100 yards away. We walked over to the spot, but just as we reached the carcase a lion sprang up and raced away. I had a shot at him but missed. He was a huge black-maned animal; one of the best I have ever seen, and I regretted not securing him. However, there was still a chance. Sending back to the wagons for the other guns, I got Hillier and Farrell to assist me in building a kraal round the carcase. We made two entrances to the kraal, and placed a gun at each, the trigger so fixed that anything crossing the opening would receive a bullet.

Having fixed up a pleasing reception for Leo, should he return during the night, we returned to the wagons, after giving old Hans instructions to remain near by till nightfall, and keep the vultures from setting on the carcase.

Hillier and myself took a couple of towels and went down to the river to have a bathe. To my great annoyance, just as we were finishing I heard one of the guns go off with a loud report.

Openly reviling old Hans for his crass stupidity, I dressed and hurried up to him, and stormed at him for disobeying my instructions and allowing the vultures to settle on the carcase and cause the gun to go off.

The old man waited till I had finished, then answered quite calmly, " I did not let the vultures pitch.   It was not the birds' doings at all, it was a lion."   I did not credit it, for four o'clock in the afternoon is an unusual time for a lion to feed, but upon going over we found the big lion there and quite dead.

After fixing up the gun again I returned to the wagons, but had not been there more than three-quarters of an hour when another report was heard. It was now almost dark, so I told the two boys and old Hans to come with me, and asked Farrell and Hillier to go over and have a look.   When we got near the trap I told them each to make a substantial torch with the dry grass, of which there was an abundance at that spot of from two to three feet high.

To the torches a match was applied, and soon the five flares were illuminating the scene.

At this moment my two dogs, magnificent bull mastiffs, who had, unknown to me, followed us out from camp, sniffed out the second lion, and commenced an attack.   The lion had only been wounded by the bullet, and when the dogs appeared on the scene, he commenced growling. At this ominous sound both the natives and the white men dropped their torches among the dry grass with quite amazing celerity, and ran to the roadway, about 100 yards away. The result was that before I reached it I was between the lion and a roaring fire—certainly as bad as being between the devil and the deep blue sea. I rushed back to try to save the two guns. One, I knew, had had its charge exploded, and this I promptly tried to rescue. I tugged and wrenched at it but could not quickly get it loose from its fastenings. By this time the flames had reached such a strength that I could see everything as plainly as in daylight. The dogs were fighting with the lion all the time, and watching my opportunity I at last got a shot in, brought the lion down, and bolted for safety, accompanied by the dogs.

Both lion skins were burned and the stock of one of the guns was also scorched. This was the only occasion up till then upon which I wished to secure the skins as trophies, and I was specially annoyed because they were the black-maned variety and very large. I had counted upon securing these to reimburse me for the loss of the oxen, for a doctor who came out with Moch, the German explorer, had offered me £7 10s. apiece for two good lion skins.

CHAPTER XVII

"NOBBY" AND THE ELEPHANTS—ELANDS AND LOCUSTS—
A CATTLE RAID—PAYING OUT M'TIBI—HOW WE "LIFTED"
HIS CATTLE—AN EXCITING TREK—A SUCCESSFUL TRIP
—I SELL UP AND SETTLE DOWN—MY OLD GUN'S AD-
VENTURES—SOME OBSERVATIONS ON BUFFALO AND
TSETSE FLY

AFTER the adventure of the two young Smidts
with the buffalo cow we remained at our temporary camp for three days for the purpose of drying
the meat. My greenhorn, " Nobby," shot a giraffe
and a couple of sable, and there was no holding
him after this. If he told me once how he did it he
told me a dozen times. He already regarded himself as a mighty hunter before the Lord, and told
me of his plans for the following year, when he
intended to come in on a hunting expedition and
shoot elephants on his own account.

Mrs. Smidt was mightily busy, metaphorically
speaking, up to her neck in the pleasant task of
boiling down fat from the numerous animals we
had slaughtered. I expected one-half of the fat so
rendered, but from the way the old lady assumed
possession, I had a shrewd notion that she regarded
it as her perquisite, and so it proved.

We got the wagons away at last, and then had a little expedition on horseback, this time taking Nobby with us. I had to impress upon him that there must be no shooting at anything save elephant, an ultimatum that chafed him considerably, seeing that we were continually passing great herds of big game. Not far from the wagons we were lucky to come across a nice herd of elephants with many young bulls among them. We each agreed to pick out our prey, and immediately we had settled this point we opened fire. I brought mine down with a bullet through the shoulder, and old Smidt was equally lucky. Following up the herd I got four more young bulls and a cow, and Smidt and his sons bagged five young bulls and six cows.

Poor Nobby got a duck's egg, for although he had struck his elephant allright, it disappeared, and despite Nobby's fond belief that it would drop within a few yards, the spoor led him and two boys for a considerable distance before it was completely obliterated by a swarm of locusts. Nobby returned to us sadly dispirited, minus ivory, and with a little experience.

By the way, I never knew before that eland would eat locusts. But they do. We watched them with our own eyes eating the insects with great relish, evidently regarding them as a rare delicacy.

I put in a good week's work at the wagons, preparing reims and sjamboks, and during this period I kept Nobby practising riding and shooting. In both pursuits he showed considerable aptitude, and when he went out and shot a couple of rhino he was distinctly pleased with himself.

We all went out the following week, but at first did very little on account of the locusts. The eggs were beginning to hatch and the ground was alive with the "voetgangers." Eventually we came across a herd of elephant, my bag amounting to nine, and the Smidts to fourteen. It took us the remainder of the week to collect the ivory, and upon our return to the wagons I put in another fortnight in cutting up and trimming whips and reims. I had over a thousand reims and about 400 whips and 300 sjamboks.

During this period of work I had several talks with Smidt concerning the wickedness of M'Tibi, who had seized my trade goods the previous year, which I had sent to him to trade for corn for my boys and cattle, and we fixed up a plan of campaign to pay the old rascal out. We agreed to start the wagons on their homeward journey in a week's time, and as we calculated that it would be a month at least before we saw the wagons again, we hid a store of coffee, sugar and tea, and a lot of "dampers" in a safe place so that we might have a supply of food upon our return to this spot. We saw the wagons safely on their way, and then we went in an opposite direction. There was myself, Nobby, Farrel, old Smidt, and his two sons, and a Cape Colony Kafir who was to act as our guide, for he was with old Hans at the time my goods were stolen. We all knew the business that was afoot, and as it was beautiful weather, and just before full moon, travelling at night was distinctly pleasant.

We arrived at M'Tibi's kraal just about sunrise on the Wednesday. We led our horses up into the hill, removed the bridles, and let them get a good feed on the grass beneath the trees.

We sat down and waited patiently expecting the cattle to come, for we had determined to take some of M'Tibi's cattle in return for my stolen goods! It was after ten o'clock before the cattle began to leave the kraals. Two herds passed our way and we resolved to secure the largest herd. We allowed them to go some distance away and then suddenly presented ourselves before the two startled boys who were in charge and told them not to attempt to escape. We fastened them together, for greater security, told them they would have to come with us for two days and then we would release them. They took the affair quite calmly; did not appear at all

alarmed and without any ado took their places behind the cattle. We started off at once, for although
we calculated that the cattle would not be missed
till nightfall upon their non-return to the kraal, we
wished to put as much distance between ourselves
and M'Tibi and his braves as we possibly could. We
kept travelling all the day and until midnight with
the briefest intervals for rest. We made another
start early on the following morning, passing below
our late camp. Two of the party went up and
secured the food we had cached, with instructions
to follow us down the river. They soon caught us
up and then we all crossed the river, trekked across
country to the next river and forded that, and here
we decided to rest for the night.

We gave our two prisoners as much meat as
they could carry and sent them back to their kraal.
The tremendous pace we had been travelling was
telling on the herd and many of the animals were
so knocked up that they could not continue the
journey and we had to leave them. Whether M'Tibi
followed us or not I do not know, but he certainly
never caught us. We got safely through the
Crocodile River, where I took sufficient cattle to
pay me for the goods that had been stolen from me
and the balance we divided, I regarding my share as
only fair recompense for all the trouble I had been
put to in connection with M'Tibi's rascality.

Leaving my cattle with a head-man there, I retraced my steps to where I had told old Hans to
wait with the wagons. I met Mrs. Smidt about 30
miles from the river, then sighted my own wagon,
where I heard a sensational story of how a herd of
cattle had been stolen from the Ma-Kalanga and
how some of the Ma-Kalanga had gone to see Seg-
koma about it! I listened with great interest but
did not enlighten them. I had been away from the
wagons for 25 days and my boys were very curious
to know where I had been. I told them a circumstantial story of how we had followed up a herd of
elephants, shot a large number, and buried the ivory,
and would take it out on the next trip.

I was very well satisfied with my short trip.
Fifty-seven elephants had fallen to my gun and the
ivory weighed close upon three thousand pounds
while, in addition, I had obtained about £300 worth
of reims, whips, sjamboks, horns, etc.

Retracing my steps to Shoshong I decided to
relinquish hunting. I had three large huts built, in
addition to the small place my brother was in, and
settled down to a trader's life. I sold my horses at
a good price and, like a stupid, parted with my old
gun. It was foolish of me, for it would have been a
great " curio," and I have regretted it ever since.
I traced it for some time. The man Horn to whom

I sold it very soon had enough of it, and parted with it to a man named Cunningham who, after having his cheek nearly knocked off by the old muzzleloader's terrific kick, sold it to a Mr. Saunders who had his eye damaged for life with it. The last white man I heard of as its proud owner was poor old Blanch, previously mentioned, who, I was informed, used to tie a three-pound bar of lead to the muzzle to keep it from jumping up, when fired. It even got too much for Blanch's nerves and at last he sold it to a Bushman, for a tusk of ivory. The old gun certainly had some peculiarities, but I had grown accustomed to them and could counteract its kick to some extent, but it always gave one a good shock and did its best to knock one out of the saddle. Still, what could one expect with a gun of that ancient pattern, whose charge was a handful of black powder and a bullet weighing something like a quarter of a pound?

I remained at Shoshong from 1870 to 1874, enjoying the rest and doing well as a trader, for I was known to everybody and there was a constantly increasing stream of hunters, explorers, etc., into the unknown and romantic north.

Before finishing the narrative of my experiences as a hunter, I cannot refrain from adding my contribution to the much-debated question of the buf-

falo. I noticed an article the other day in one of
our local papers in which reference was made to the
" unsportsmanlike " behaviour of some buffalo
hunters in North-Western Rhodesia in not following up wounded buffalo, when they withdrew into
a swamp. The writer of the article must have been
supremely ignorant of the buffalo and his ways for
I think it was eminently sensible of those hunters
not to follow up wounded buffalo into a place where
they had lots of cover. Far better follow up a
wounded lion than a wounded buffalo, for the latter is the fiercest and most cunning animal to be
found in Africa. The German Lieutenant Graetz
and his companions have recently discovered that
fact, for one of them has been killed and Lieutenant
Graetz severely injured through following up a
wounded buffalo. No, a man who is out after
buffalo must shoot to kill and not to wound, and if
he fails to bring his quarry down he should on no
account venture to follow up unless in open country.
He should never follow a buffalo into cover, unless
he is accompanied by a number of good dogs. Many
a good man has lost his life through neglect of this
precaution.

In connection with buffalo I should like to add
my mite to the tsetse-fly controversy and the association of the fly with the buffalo. I can mention

three large tracts of country which were once infested with the fly. There was a belt on the Crocodile River close to Tuli; also the place where Khama has his village to-day, and a third area around the Victoria Falls. In all three places buffalo and tsetse-fly were, literally, found in swarms. To-day there are no buffalo and no fly in either district. I feel bound to accept the testimony of the natives on this point, and they assert that the fly breeds in the buffalo dung. Once the buffalo is eradicated the fly disappear, as they have no breeding place.

I am bound to say this, from my own experience, that it is possible to get fly at distances up to sixty to seventy miles away from the run of the buffalo, the pests being carried out of the usual " fly-belt " by other game.

The buffalo on the Crocodile River were shot and driven out by trek Boers. Three large families of Boers were standing at the junction of the Marico and Crocodile Rivers for over a year, and we all know what a vast quantity of game they would shoot in that time.

CHAPTER XVIII

THE FINAL TRIP—A GUN-RUNNING EXPEDITION—TEMPTED
BY DIAMONDS—CANNON FOR SECOCONI—ARRESTED BY
BOERS—A TIGHT CORNER—HOW WE TRICKED OUR
CAPTORS

IN 1875 I purchased from Port Elizabeth three
old ship's cannons, having in view what I thought
would prove a profitable, if somewhat risky, little
adventure. I transported them up to Grahamstown, and from there to Kimberley.

The little project I had in mind was to run them
into Secoconi's country, in the Northern Transvaal.
Three of Secoconi's boys had been working for me
for some time, and they were always dropping hints
to me that Secoconi was extremely anxious to obtain
a big gun, and that if he could only get one into his
country to help him against the Boers he would give
the man who was able to bring it in the whole of his
diamonds. As it was rumoured that Secoconi had
a big stock of diamonds—how or where obtained I
do not know—it seemed to me good enough to
attempt the spec.

I had heard many stories of Secoconi's hoard of
diamonds—and many legends have grown up
around this alleged wealth—some people speaking

of pots of diamonds, others bags, but, generally, there was an idea abroad that Secoconi's diamonds were worth considerably more than a king's ransom. At any rate it was good enough for me to try and get them, in return for a couple of cannon.

My brother was with me. We had three wagons and purchased a quantity of guns and ammunition. Amongst the guns were some very good weapons— the best that were to be purchased in those days— and we knew very well that we could obtain a high price for them in the interior. We obtained a permit from the Transvaal Government to proceed with " arms and ammunition " from their territory into " Kafirland." The permit did not say anything with regard to the guns as to number or size; in fact, nothing beyond the phrase " arms and ammunition." We therefore thought that we were fully armed with the necessary authority, though I may here say that the cannon was carefully hidden from sight.

When we started on our expedition we decided to make the attempt with only one of the cannon, leaving the other two at Kimberley for the time being, for I felt that if we were successful with the first, there would be no need to take the other up, while if our first attempt was frustrated in any way, there were still two more in reserve at a convenient jumping-off spot. There was, therefore, the chance that I would be able to get at least one out of the three up to old Secoconi. The method of concealing the one cannon that I took up was firmly to strap it to the bed of a cart and cover the whole vehicle with a false floor. The work was neatly carried out, all fastened down with screws, and there was not much possibility of any prying eyes detecting the fact that there was anything in the cart.

We went quietly along the edge of the Transvaal to the point I had made up my mind as the most convenient place to make the dash into Secoconi's country. This spot was about 12 hours westward from Rustenburg. We outspanned here, and while we were resting, preparatory to the move out of the Boer's country, we were dismayed by the arrival on the scene of six armed Boers who rode up and, without any ado, demanded our business, and whether we had in our possession a big gun—a cannon.

"Yes," said my brother, with what I thought unnecessary impudence.

"Where is it?" asked the leader of the party.

My brother, with an offhand air, said: "It is tied up in the tent." The Boers demanded to be shown it immediately. We walked to the tent, and my brother calmly pointed to an old swivel duck-gun, with a bell-shaped mouth, which was hanging there.

I nearly burst with laughter at this piece of cheek, but dared not show it. The Dutchmen, who saw that they had been made fun of, were very angry, and the leader savagely turned upon my brother, and asked him if he thought he was a fool to make him believe that that old duck-gun was a cannon?

My brother, who had not moved a muscle of his face throughout the incident, answered quite innocently that the Boers had asked if we had literally a "big gun" and he in his innocence had shown them the only big gun we possessed.

The Boer said, angrily, "I don't mean a gun like that. I mean a large weapon (kanon)." He then added: "Where are you going to?"

"Into Kafirland," said my brother.

"Have you got a permit?" was the next question.

"Yes," answered my brother, and we produced the permit I have previously mentioned, giving us permission to bring "arms and ammunition" through the Transvaal.

The leader took it. In spite of being a Dutchman he was no fool, and he quickly noticed a fact, which we had entirely overlooked, that the permit bore no date. It had been made out by Landdrost Best at Christiana, and he had carelessly omitted to date it. Otherwise the permit was entirely in order. However, the Boers were evidently looking for trouble, were quick to spot the omission and promptly placed us under arrest.

We all sat down and had a long palaver, talked the matter over in all its bearings, smoked our pipes, had a liquor, and generally comported ourselves with the ease and leisureliness of men whose lives were spent on the veld. There was no need for hurry on their part for they were out on a big expedition—there could be nothing more imposing to the Boers' mind than to arrest " Verdomde Englesmen " for such a terrible offence as running a big gun through their country to be used against them. At that stage of the country's history it must have been as sensational an affair as the Jameson Raid was in later years.

It was quite evident to me that the Boers' secret service further down country was fairly good, because although I had taken every precaution to ensure absolute secrecy with regard to the cannon, some one evidently had " given the show away." There was no doubt our movements had been watched all the way up-country, and just as we were about to cross the border the Boers were awaiting us. The very fact that they insisted that we had a big cannon in our possession showed that they were not going to be easily bluffed, and feeling this I certainly was not in a hurry to cut the conversation short until some scheme of outwitting them had crossed my mind. I knew that I should have to exercise all my ingenuity to get out of the very tight hole in which we were placed, for the Boers had no love for a man who was attempting to do as I calculated to do.

At last they said: "How far are you going to-night?"

We replied that we would not go very far and would only make a short trek that day, adding, which was quite true, that we were in no hurry to get further into the Transvaal.

They said we would have to come to some arrangement with regard to the position, adding that they did not wish to be under the necessity of putting us all under formal arrest and making us their prisoners as they had been instructed to do. They added, parenthetically as it were, that they had been instructed to intercept us by President Burgers, the then president of the Republic, who had ordered them not to stand on ceremony but that, upon finding the cannon in our possession, they were to hang us to the nearest trees!

This was a pretty state of affairs, to say the least of it, for while I knew the Boers would take very serious notice of our action if we were caught I thought, knowing them as I did, that we would be able to get off at the very worst with a considerable fine, and this statement that they were instructed to hang us to the nearest trees was a by no means pleasant reflection.

Having cheered our drooping spirits in this way the Boers said they had no wish to be unduly harsh at this stage and so, if we would agree as to our conduct, etc., we were free to go on our way, of course accompanied by our friendly guards.

The leader said he didn't want to go very far that day and advised us not to go beyond the next farm, which was quite sufficient trek for that day, being about five miles off.

I replied, " Very well." We proceeded on our way but I made an excuse to outspan before we got there. I was not at all anxious to get close to any Boer farm at the present juncture.

When we outspanned we did so at a spot very carefully selected by me. During the five miles of trek I had been anxiously trying to discover some scheme whereby I might outwit the Boers and save my neck, and at last I saw something that gave me a hope. I was riding ahead of the wagons and suddenly dropped back, ordered them to out-span, but, altering my usual procedure at camping time, I did not have the wagons drawn up close together. The three wagons were in a line some considerable distance apart, while at one end of the line was the cart. From one end of the line to the other must have been 50 yards, if not more.

At the end of the line opposite to that occupied by the cart I made camp for ourselves. I had a large quantity of soft grass cut and spread around in the form of a bed, near the wagons. I threw upon this a number of blankets, skins, etc., and it made a luxurious couch fit for a king. This couch I placed at the disposal of our Dutch captors and they settled themselves upon its yielding surface with an air of luxury and contentment that was pleasing to behold.

While the camp fire was being lighted and the coffee boiled my brother Harry slipped away from the wagons with our three pointer dogs, ostensibly to see if he could get a few birds or buck for food, but really to see whether there were any other people around us. They were first-class pointers, good at their work and it did not take him many minutes to discover that our camp was surrounded by a whole ring of natives who had been concealing themselves in the thick grass and bush. He ascertained that they were not necessarily hostile to white men as a whole, but that they were in the employ of the Boers and that they had surrounded us from the moment when the Boers came on the scene that morning and had been keeping alongside the wagons the whole day. They now formed a complete cordon round the camp so that there was very little hope in attempting to escape.

I quickly made up my mind what to do. When the coffee was boiling I poured a bottle of Three-star French brandy into the kettle, put plenty of sugar in it—knowing the Dutchman's love of sweet things—produced some biscuit and served round the evening meal. My word, but you should have seen how they drank that coffee! They even complimented me upon its nice taste, and when the kettle had been emptied they settled back on the couch of grass with their pipes in their mouths, contented with themselves and all the world, happy in the consciousness that they had secured the notorious gun-runners and that they were surrounded by a ring of argus-eyed natives from whom nothing could escape.

I could read their thoughts pretty clearly and so in order to make doubly sure I suggested that they might like a drop of brandy.

Brandy! Of course they would like a brandy.

Was there ever a Dutchman who refused a drop of liquor when out on the veld? I knew my Dutchmen too well to imagine that I should have any difficulty in inducing them to take as much liquor as I could offer them. Going to the wagon I produced another bottle—the first so far as they knew—and served out fine, healthy tots all round.

The double rations of liquor soon began to have their effect. First the Dutchmen grew talkative, then more or less hilarious, then slightly argumentative and finally first one and then the other showed signs of sleep. Needless to say we encouraged them in this by yawning and showing every symptom of drowsiness and these suggestions in time had their effect and the Dutchmen gently sank into slumber.

This was what we were waiting for.

CHAPTER XIX

TRICKING THE BOERS—HOW WE HID THE CANNON—AND
COVERED OUR TRACKS—ARRIVAL IN RUSTENBURG—
BEFORE THE LANDDROST

OUR apparently sleepy eyes were quickly opened. We crept away from the camp fire as quietly as possible and hurried to the rear of the wagon line where the cart was stationed.

There was now no fear of the native cordon of spies around us since my brother Harry with the three big pointers had put the fear of God into their hearts and chased them back to a distance of a mile or more from our camp.

We immediately commenced to put my scheme into operation. I had camped at this particular spot because, riding along at the head of the wagons, I had noticed some native game-pits and had carefully drawn the wagons up in such a manner that the cart was nearly opposite to them. The idea I had in view was to outspan, as I had done, near to the pits, to get the Dutchmen drunk, and while they were asleep to take out the bottom of the cart, hide the cannon in one of the game-pits, and then, with an easy conscience, we could face further in-

vestigation, because so long as there was no cannon
on board there could not possibly be any hanging
or any further trouble. The game-pits were in the
form of a half-moon, in extent about 300 yards,
having been dug out by natives for the purpose of
catching game. Each hole was about two feet across
and with a depth of about six feet. All the holes
were on the opposite side of the road from where
we had made camp, I having carefully drawn my
wagons into a clearing on the opposite side of the
road so that the Dutchmen would not see the game
pits unless they were more than usually inquisitive.

When we reached the cart I loosened the four
oxen that were attached to its disselboom and woke
up a young fellow named Slade who had joined
our party some few days earlier.

I said to him: " Get up, man, and give us a hand.
I am in a mess."

" What's the matter? " he asked.

" Don't talk, man," I said, " Come and help. I
have got something on board that I am not sup-
posed to have."

" By God! I thought so," was his reply.

" Never mind what you think," was my retort,
" but come and give me a hand."

Slade was all right. He promptly turned out,
and the three of us, one at the pole and one at each

wheel, quietly moved the cart across the road to the game-pits, about 300 yards off. We got into the cart and with screw drivers loosened the planking, pulled it all out, unfastened the lashings of the gun and prepared to unship it. I was at the muzzle end of the gun while my brother and Slade were at the other end and it was agreed that at the " one, two, three " they were to give the hoist. The programme was faithfully carried out, but we had not allowed for the action of heaving a gun in a cart on two wheels. At the word " three " they gave the heave, but the two being heavier than myself the pole of the cart, which of course was resting on the ground, shot straight up into the air, throwing the cart right back and hurling the three of us sprawling to the ground.

Luckily for us, owing to the darkness we had not loosened all the lashings, or the gun, as well as ourselves, would have come flying out and possibly one if not more of us might have been very seriously injured. As it was the incident was only a laughable one and we proceeded to make another attempt. I told Slade to sit on the disselboom and I and Harry would try to lift the gun simultaneously or, at any rate, push it out of the cart.

We pulled the cart again into position with the pole on the ground and Slade sat on the point of it.

I was standing straddlewise across the gun, my brother at the end. Once more the word was given, " one, two, three," and at the hoist we both lifted together and with such good will that the gun came out, the big butt end caught me between the legs and hurled me out of the cart with it, almost on to the top of Slade.

The whole incident was too much for us and we all burst out into a yell of laughter that must have been heard far beyond the spot where the Boers were peacefully sleeping. If they had not been, I won't say drunk, but very near it, they would have heard our laughter and investigated it, for it must not be forgotten that we also had taken a fair quantity of the brandy and were in a decidedly careless and reckless mood. Once we had started laughing we didn't worry who heard it until our laugh was over when, of course, we realised the necessity for extreme caution.

We listened intently and turned anxious glances towards the end of the wagon-line where the fitful gleams of the camp-fire showed the Dutchmen peacefully sleeping. There was no movement and if either of them was disturbed by our noise he made no sign. After satisfying ourselves that our untimely laughter had had no evil consequences we promptly proceeded to negotiate the cannon, which we dropped down one of the game-pits and carefully concealed its mouth with a big old thorn-bush whose stump we thrust down into the hole. We imagined it would take a clever eye to detect that the tree had not actually grown there, while with the arrival of the rains and the growth of the grass we calculated that it was good for at least two years unless destroyed by fire.

We carefully replaced the floor of the cart, splashboard, etc., and here I was more than grateful that I had the foresight to have the whole of this work done with such care that it could be put in or taken out without hammering or breaking the boards, and that a screw-driver was all that was needed to effect the change.

It was now between one and two o'clock in the morning, and, so far, everything had gone off satisfactorily. We pulled the cart back to its original position, and I told my brother and Slade to turn in and get some sleep. I, however, had something further to do to make all secure. Knowing what a particularly keen eye the Dutchman has for spoor I realised that the cart-tracks across the road would be quickly picked up in the morning unless I took steps completely to obliterate them. My plan I had already formed, and now proceeded to put it into execution. Going up to the wagons where the oxen were fastened, I set them all loose, and rousing two of my most trustworthy boys to help me we quickly had the oxen together.

Just at this juncture I was startled to see one of the Boers prop himself on his elbow and ask sleepily, but yet suspiciously, " You are not going to inspan now, are you? "

" No," I responded equally sleepily, " but I forgot that when we outspanned last night I tied the oxen up instead of letting them graze, and we had such a good time drinking brandy that I forgot all about the poor beasts, so I am letting them loose now to get some food, otherwise we shall have to wait two or three hours in the morning before we can inspan! "

" Ja, mynheer," he said, and dropped back upon his couch, evidently quite satisfied with my explanation.

I and the boys promptly drove the oxen to the spot between the game-pit where we had dropped the cannon and where the cart was stationed. We drove them backwards and forwards and once or twice across it, completely obliterating every vestige of wheel tracks. When I had done this to my satisfaction I tied them up to the wagons, turned in and went to sleep with an easy conscience and a profound feeling of innocence and rectitude! I didn't

open my eyes till well after sunrise—so soundly
does a man sleep with a clear conscience—but when
at last I awoke I found that the Boers had been
awake before me some considerable time, and that
two of them had gone off on horseback to report
us to the magistrate at Rustenburg, while the others
had evidently being prying around the wagons to
see what they could see. However, they gave no
symptoms of having discovered anything suspicious,
and we inspanned and travelled for about a mile
and a half, when we came to a rivulet on the other
side of which was a farm house, the property of
Paul Krüger's son-in-law. We arrived here on
Saturday, and were instructed that we must remain
at this spot until the messengers returned from
Rustenburg, with instructions as to what was to be
done with us. Of course, I assumed an air of injured innocence, and wanted to know what they
meant by holding up inoffensive traders in this
fashion, seeing that we had no big cannon on board.
In fact, I challenged them to produce the cannon,
and threatened them with all sorts of pains and
penalties, actions for damages and so on, if they
didn't let us go.

Meantime, however, we didn't have a bad time,
for we went out shooting, and, for the first time in
their lives these Dutchmen saw well-trained pointers

at work. They were simply amazed at the clever-
ness of the dogs, and at the results obtained when
out shooting. There was one particular small patch
of ground at the bottom of the land, and I suppose
we must have shot 30 to 40 pheasants there at one
expedition. We gave all the birds to the Dutchmen, and they were highly delighted. They were
amazed at the rapidity with which the birds fell to
our guns, and said they had never seen anything
like it in their lives. I should add that on this occasion we were using breech-loaders. These useful
weapons had now been introduced, and the old
muzzle-loader with which I had had such famous
sport in my time was a thing of the past. The
breech-loader had taken its place, and this was the
first occasion upon which I had put it to a practical
test. Of course, in those days it was a great novelty,
and to the Boers it was entirely new. I had a large
number of breech-loading rifles on the wagons, and
it was because of their novelty and efficiency that I
anticipated making a quite good thing out of their
sale, apart from disposing of the cannon.

On Sunday night the Boers returned from
Rustenburg with orders that we were to be taken
to the Landdrost there, and that they were not to
do anything until we arrived at that famous Dutch
dorp. I knew perfectly well once we got there that

our wagons would be overhauled, particularly as the
messengers from Rustenburg made it perfectly
clear that the Boers meant business, and that President Burger's instructions would be carried out in
the event of our being found guilty. True, I had
got rid of the cannon, but there were a few other
little things on the wagons connected with the
weapon that might put us away. One of these was
a big brass mould for casting solid balls for the gun.
I had this mould specially made by a brass founder
in Grahamstown, who, by the way, charged me £7
10s. for the job. It was a good mould, however, and
a big and conspicuous piece of work. I imagined
that if the Boers found this upon my wagon, they
would go back and search every inch of my trail
until they picked up the cannon. Then there were
some heavy castings to form the carriage of the
gun. These also were on the wagons, together with
the wheels, and the question was how to get rid of
them?

I took counsel with my brother, and told him
that, above all, these things must be got rid of that
night. It was our only hope, and we must devise a
plan for disposing of them.

He said: " Why not throw them into that pool
of water there, when the Boers are asleep? "

This we decided to do, and late that night, when

everything was quiet, we pitched the iron-work of the gun carriage, the brass mould and everything connected with the cannon into the mud-hole. It looked to me as though it contained permanent water, and I imagined that these heavy metal articles would sink into the mud and remain there concealed until the Day of Judgment. In this, however, I was wrong as the sequel will show, but of this more later. For the moment it was out of sight, and we went forward with the Boers to Rustenburg with a light heart.

We reached Rustenburg on the Wednesday night, and were brought before the old Magistrate there on the following morning. I cannot remember his name—and I don't think he could write it himself—but he was not such a bad old sort. I was the first to be called before him. The first question put was: " Do the wagons belong to you? "

I replied, " No, they belong to my brother. I only came up with him on a trip. All I have got is the little cart and four horses. What I really came up for was to have a little shooting on the Crocodile River, and after that I shall return to Kimberley. The wagons and everything else belong to my brother."

"Ah," he said, " you are not the man we want.

We don't want you at all. We want the man who owns the wagons," and he told me to stand down.

Then Slade and my brother were called up, and were charged with having guns, including a big cannon, without authority. We all acknowledged having guns and ammunition, also a hogshead of brandy and other trading stuff on the wagons, but denied all knowledge of a big cannon, and produced our permits to show that we had authority for bringing the rifles and ammunition in.

CHAPTER XX

OUTWITTING THE MAGISTRATE—MY ESCAPE FROM RUSTEN-
BURG—"INTO THE LION'S DEN"—AN EARLY MORNING
FRIGHT—A DASH FOR THE SOUTH—THE LION AND THE
BLANKET—THE FUNNIEST FIGHT ON EARTH

THE Magistrate heard the evidence, such as it
was, and while he kindly told me that I could go as I
evidently had nothing to do with the ownership of
the wagons, remanded my brother and Slade. I
promptly asked him for a passport. This he refused
to give at first, saying that he didn't see why I
wanted one.

Luckily for me I could speak Dutch like a
Dutchman, when I wanted to. Addressing the
Landdrost in his own tongue and speaking as good
Taal as any burgher, I said: "Look here, Your Worship, I carry the same name as this notorious brother
of mine who owns these wagons. He has been
arrested on a very serious charge, a very serious
charge indeed, as all good burghers know. Now
you acknowledge that I am free, that the charge
has nothing whatever to do with me and that I have
nothing to do with his affairs, or with you. Now
suppose I go away to the north and I come up
against one of your Field-Cornets and he says to me:

'What is your name?' I reply, 'Finaughty.'
He will say to me, 'You are the man who was
arrested for running a big gun into the Transvaal.'
I say to him, 'But that is my brother.' He will
immediately reply, 'No, you are the man, you have
no brother, but you have escaped from custody and
I shall now arrest you and take you back to Rustenburg.' I continued: "Don't you see, Your Worship,
that unless you give me a passport I shall be liable
to be turned back wherever I go and I shall be put
to a great deal of suffering and trouble. Besides,
I am not going to stay in the Transvaal. I am only
on a short trip and must get back to Kimberley
quickly, otherwise my business will suffer. Now
then, Your Worship, if I can show the Field-Cornets
a free pass from you they will allow me to go on my
way, and so I want you to give it to me."

I could see that the old man was favourably
impressed by my argument, but there was a touch of
reluctance about him. I promptly turned to the
Government Prosecutor (upon whom I had spent a
fairly large sum in the shape of drinks, from the
moment we arrived in Rustenburg, and could therefore count upon him as being more or less friendly!)
and said, "You know what I say is right. Speak
up for me and tell His Worship that my argument
is good law and good sense."

The Public Prosecutor replied, "Yes, Your Worship, he is perfectly right and he will have great trouble outside if you don't give him this passport."

The Landdrost was by this time convinced, ordered the clerk to make out the passport, which was handed to me and I was released.

When I got back to the wagons I found that the five Boers had been sleeping in them and that they were surrounded by a ring of natives to see that neither of us got away nor anything connected with the wagons.

With my passport in my hand I was able to assert myself, and promptly proceeded to get my two-seated buggy in order. I picked out the four best horses, got the harness together, and when the Boer guard were not looking I managed to obtain from the wagons a quantity of ammunition, a shot-gun and a Westley-Richards fall-block rifle. I also obtained about 600 rounds of ammunition, and loaded the whole of it into the cart. The two boys who had assisted me with the oxen in obliterating the marks of the cart at the time I secreted the cannon, were too dangerous to leave behind, because I knew the Boers had a way of extracting information and I didn't care to take any chances, so having inspanned the horses I bundled the two niggers into the cart and set off away to the west, taking with me a couple of spare horses alongside, out of the total number of eight we had brought up with us.

It was a beautiful moonlight night, and I got away unobserved about 3 o'clock in the morning. I put the horses to it at top speed and did not stop till daylight, when I outspanned for a few hours. I then inspanned again, and was trekking along as fast as I could go when, coming over a rise, a Dutchman's house came into view. At the time I didn't know whose it was, but on the clear fresh morning air the scent of grilled mutton came rising up on the breeze. I really ought to have continued my journey, but the smell of grilled chops after my long night's trek was too much for me, and telling the boys to outspan, I turned into the homestead in the hope of getting some breakfast. To my amazement I found I had run right into the farm-house of the Field-Cornet who, of course, knew all about my arrest. However, there was no help for it. I had put my head right into the lion's mouth again and must take the risk.

They were very hospitable, asked me to have some breakfast, and I can assure you that I never enjoyed mutton chops so much in all my life.

While I was having breakfast I noticed a Boer lad, a mere stripling, occasionally glance at me; but at the moment I didn't take much notice. Shortly afterwards I heard him talking to the boys, and then realised that he was one of the Boers who had formed part of the escort into Rustenberg, but had returned immediately upon our arrival there, and had only just got back to the farmhouse. He was telling a most circumstantial story to the other Boers about a big gun that they had found which the Englishmen had brought into the country, but had hidden. He was explaining to them, with a wealth of detail, how he had found it, described what a great big gun it was, and with his hands showed that it had a " great mouth like that."

To say that the disclosure made me a trifle uneasy is to put it mildly, but, listening a little further, to my relief I found that the boy was nothing but a first-class liar, that he knew nothing whatever about any big gun, excepting what he had been told, and that he was indulging in the usual Boer bravado and lying in order to show his comrades what a fine fellow he was.

While this conversation was going on, and the whole of us were listening to the yarn, I became so disgusted with the youngster's lies that I said abruptly, " Don't believe him; he is telling lies."

The old man said: " Hush, be careful, and don't say too much," adding, " I am the Field-Cornet of this district, and you had better tell me what you are doing here."

I showed him my passport, which he carefully examined, and said, " Yes, that's all right." I did not stay very long after this. I was too near danger to consider myself at all comfortable, and I promptly inspanned, apologised for my hurry, and went away as fast as the horses could travel.

Two hours later I met two young English farmers whom I had met before. I exchanged one of my horses for a salted horse that they had and gave them my cheque for £40, on Kimberley, for the exchange.

I drove all that night till I got through the Crocodile River. Early next morning I inspanned and moved steadily down the Crocodile, where I came across a Boer camp. Here I had a weird adventure. I was very fond of one of my horses and used to take particular care of him, especially at night, to protect him from accident or disease. He was wrapped in one of my blankets every night and on this occasion I covered him with a big white woollen blanket fastened at the throat with a small piece of thin twine, and a girth over him also fastened with a piece of thin twine. I did this so that in the event of him becoming entangled in any bushes the twine would easily break and the horse would be released. This little piece of thoughtfulness saved his life that night.

Shortly after midnight I was suddenly aroused by a horse's scream of terror, and springing up I saw in the moonlight a whirl of dust at the spot where the horse had been standing. Almost at the same moment I heard the snap of a reim and then out of the dust my horse came running towards me minus the blanket. Seizing my gun I fired at the spot he had just left but whether my bullet took effect I could not tell. Having captured the horse— I had to run a quarter of a mile after him—I tied him up and then went to look for the lion and my white blanket. Neither was to be seen, but next morning a short distance away I found the blanket clawed and bitten in the most extraordinary manner. There was not a piece as large as the palm of one's hand that was not full of teeth and claw marks. A most extraordinary thing appeared to have happened.

It was clear that the lion had sprung upon the horse, for there was a four-inch wound in his thigh— but the blanket had proved his undoing. As the lion's claws fastened themselves into the blanket the weight of the beast and the startled jump of the horse had caused the flimsy fastenings to snap, with the result that the lion had fallen to the ground with the blanket over him!

He evidently had an extraordinary fight before he managed to free himself from its clinging folds. There were signs that he had rolled all over the place and, as I have already stated, he had bitten and torn the blanket in a hundred places; in fact there was scarcely any blanket left, only a mess of rags and shreds.

If I had not been in pursuit of my horse I should have witnessed the funniest sight it was ever given a hunter to see—a fight to the death between a lion and a blanket! What the lion thought of it all I cannot tell, but there is very little doubt that despite his desperate encounter he had a very poor supper out of the blanket and was very glad, in the finish, to leave the remnants of his enemy in possession of the field.

CHAPTER XXI

A LUCKY ESCAPE—CHASED BY A COMMANDO—ONLY A FEW
HOURS' START—OXEN FOR HORSES—ANOTHER CANNON
EXPEDITION—ARRIVAL AT BULAWAYO—PURCHASED BY
LOBENGULA

PROCEEDING on my way southwards with all
possible expedition, I reached the Crocodile River
and crossed, thence to the Marico River. Having
reached the southern bank of the last mentioned,
I continued along the course of the river for some
distance, making for Kimberley. At 'Mtwani I
came across a white trader and to him I sold my
four tired horses receiving in exchange six young
oxen. These I inspanned in the cart in the place
of the horses and they carried me along at a much
faster pace. It is surprising how fast fresh oxen
can travel with only a light load behind them and
I was more than gratified at the excellent pace they
made and the manner in which they extended the
distance between myself and my quondam Boer
friends! Although I had my passport I was by no
means sure that the Rustenburg magistrate would
not repent of his decision and send out orders to
have me detained and taken back.

It was lucky for me that I made such expedition

out of the country for I afterwards heard that on
the morning following my quiet but hurried departure from Rustenburg, the magistrate ordered
out a commando, forty strong, to overtake me and
bring me back a prisoner. The messengers he had
despatched to Pretoria with news of the arrest of
the gun-runners had returned post-haste with a mes-
sage from President Burgers that we were all to
be taken immediately to Pretoria. Unfortunately
for them, but luckily for me, I had departed a few
hours earlier. Even when they found I had outwitted them and the commando was ordered out,
there was considerable delay and confusion. Some
could not get horses; those who had horses could
not procure saddles, while those who had both horses
and saddles were without rifles and ammunition!
By the time they were all fitted up it was nine
o'clock, but with the start I had secured they had
no chance, barring accidents, of catching me up.
I imagine that they returned somewhat disconsolate
at being duped by an Englishman.

But to resume. I went considerably faster with
the oxen than I had gone with the horses and never
stopped trotting the whole of the first day, for they
had nothing to speak of to pull and, being only
half-trained, they were full of spirit. I made my
way in the direction of Kanya, where I met Selous

for the first time, though I believe he had been in once before. It was here I sold him the salted horse I had previously purchased from Topper. If I remember rightly, Selous gave me £90 for him; at any rate it was certainly a very high price, for he was exceptionally big and strong and in perfect condition.

From here I made my way quietly to Kimberley, which I reached without further adventure.

After a rest I began to make my preparations to move the two cannon I had left here. I purchased a wagon and oxen, and obtained a permit to proceed, with guns and ammunition, into the interior on a hunting trip (of course). My next move was to load the two cannon up so that the authorities would not be any the wiser—a by no means easy task. First of all I loaded them, covered by the other stuff, upon the wagon of a Boer who lived at Heilbron, told him to use a red flag to show there was gunpowder on board and to proceed to Heilbron and await me there.

When I arrived I heard that his wagon was standing outside Heilbron and when I went to him and asked him why he did not bring the wagon to the other side of the town close up to mine, he began whimpering and blubbering like a baby and said he had had an awful ride, and did not know what he was carrying, and he wouldn't have taken the job on if he had known it, and so on and so forth.

I was not long in tumbling to what was in his mind. I said, " You know perfectly well you are telling lies. You knew all along what you were carrying because you carried my permit. You were carrying guns and ammunition and a couple of old pumps."

" They're very funny pumps with touch-holes in them? " he enquired, with a sly look in his moist, crafty eyes and added with a burst of crying, "And I have just lost a brother in Secoconi's country where I suppose these guns are going to enable him to kill my relatives and other upright Boers! "

" Look here McGrauw," I replied, " I know what's troubling you. Not your conscience nor the loss of your alleged brother, nor the loss of some upright burghers, but you are looking to make more out of me for a bit of risky business. Well, I will give you another £10 to bring them up to my wagon."

This soon dried his tears, and he promised readily to bring them along, but when he did so, and I with the aid of a couple of white pals had got the cannons on to my wagons, I gave him a fiver and kicked him out of my camp, for his rapacity.

I rode night and day till I got out of Griqualand. It took me three full days and nights to get over the border, which I did on the morning of the fourth day. My oxen, as might be expected were terribly distressed at such a long spell of heavy work, and I had intended to give them a good spell to rest and recuperate; but they took matters into their own hands, ran away and left me and could not be found for a fortnight, despite the most tempting rewards. At last some natives brought them back, but they were so tired they would scarcely move.

However, we made a move at last and reached Kanya, where I had to wait for three other wagons which my brother Harry was to bring along.

I must here explain that my brother and Slade had been released from custody. After their arrival at Pretoria, President Burgers and the Boers there finding no cannons on the wagons, and being faced with the permit to carry arms and ammunition, were unable to do anything. They, however, turned a loving eye upon the fine stock of rifles in the wagons, and ultimately made an offer to purchase the rifles and ammunition at a high price. Unfortunately this was at the historical time when there was no money in the Transvaal treasury, and though my brother wanted cash, he also wanted to get out of their clutches, and so accepted a bill for six months at 11 per cent.

We proceeded to the Marico where I bought 400 head of oxen from a man named Taylor. Some of them had been inoculated and many were sick. I handed them over to my brother and told him to trade them off at a profit of 50 per cent., a reasonable enough figure in those days. He went down country with the oxen and one wagon, while I sold one wagon and started northwards with two, in one of them being the two cannon.

At Shoshong I did a little trading, and while resting here was amused by the receipt of a letter from my brother in which he informed me that he had camped by the mud-hole wherein we had hidden the brass mould and the iron carriage and fittings of the first cannon, and that instead of them sinking out of human sight forever and a day, as we had hoped, what was my brother's amazement to find that the water had all dried up, that the mud was hard, and that the local Boers had taken possession of the big brass mould which, when the water dried up, stood up unblushingly in the middle of the pond! But this was not all; they were so convinced that the cannon was also there that they reported the matter to President Burgers, who, angry at letting the " gun-runners " escape him, sent out a huge gang of natives to dig out the mud and produce the *corpus delicti!*

When my brother arrived they had made a huge excavation some 40 feet deep, but all they had found was the iron portions of the carriage, and never having seen the like before, they did not know what it was. Naturally, my brother did not enlighten them, and as they could not re-arrest him on the strength of the brass mould, they had to content themselves with threats of what they would do *when* they found the cannon.

But they didn't find it, and shortly after this date, when the Transvaal was annexed by the British Government, my brother presented his bill for the rifles and ammunition; it was honoured by the British, who gave him a draft upon Cape Town, and in the course of time the money was forthcoming. This was excellent, and made the first big-gun running expedition a profitable little venture, even if it did not eventuate in a fortune, as I had hoped.

But to return to the other two cannon. After having slipped out of the Boer noose once I was not going to risk it a second time, so made up my mind to give Secoconi the go-by, and to bring in the two cannon to Lobengula. I arrived at Old Bulawayo in 1876 where Lo Ben received me cordially. He had heard the story of my arrest by the Boers and was frankly nonplussed, not to say disappointed with me. He said he could not under-

stand how the famous " Billy " that he formerly
knew, " who used to destroy all my big game and
my elephants," and think nothing of it, allowed half
a dozen Boers to take him a prisoner. He told me
that when he heard of it he could not believe it.

He looked me up and down in an incredulous
manner and then burst out laughing, in which he
was heartily joined by his sister, both of whom frequently treated the matter as a huge joke. I had
a big feed of meat with him in his hut and we sat
talking over old times. Then he sent for some very
excellent beer—mealie beer sweetened with honey—
and told me, with a sly look, not to drink too much.

" Why, King? " I asked innocently.

" Because if you do," he remarked sententiously,
" you will have a very bad head—I know." At which
we both laughed heartily.

On returning to my wagons, I gave him a case
of sparkling cider, but called " champagne," as a
present and told him there wasn't a headache in
the whole case. It looked good and tasted as good
as it looked, and the old man appreciated it as much
as if it had been the real thing. Having put him
into a good humour, I got one Jack Deans, who
was with me, to introduce the subject of the big
guns, as I did not then wish my name to be mixed
up with the transaction. He did not make a par-

ticularly good bargain. All he could obtain for them was about £190 worth of ivory.

We left the guns there and they remained unused, lying near Lobengula's hut until the Occupation, and the flight of Lobengula, when they were hidden, to be unearthed some two years ago and presented to the Bulawayo Museum. They now lie, rusted and neglected, outside the main entrance of that institution, without even a block of wood under them to show them off. As for the cannon I dropped down the game pit, I never bothered further about it, but I afterwards heard that a cannon had been found down that way and was in the possession of a native chief for many years and that it was afterwards taken to Mafeking and did duty at the famous siege of that town, subsequently to find an honoured place among the relics of the siege. I do not know if it was my old gun or not—but the facts seem to fit together.

CHAPTER XXII

AN IVORY DEAL—AFTER ELEPHANTS WITH BREECH-
LOADERS—A PAINFUL EXPERIENCE—A COWARDLY DOG
—A USEFUL ELEPHANT "BAG"—ADVENTURE WITH A
LIONESS—A TERRIBLE ENCOUNTER—MY BOY BADLY
MAULED

I MAY mention that I did not come in on this
trip solely for the purpose of selling the two old
ship's guns. My object was to combine business
with pleasure, so to speak, and to make it a profitable
trading trip as far as possible. Beyond the small
quantity of ivory Lobengula paid for the cannon,
he had none available for trading purposes, much
as he said he would have liked to do a deal. He said
if I wanted oxen he would trade my stuff, but I
replied that it was too far to drive them and, furthermore, that I was in a hurry.

On my arrival at Mangwe I obtained a nice
parcel of ivory from John Lee, paying him £300
or £400 cash. I also sold him a salted horse and
some muskets. Leaving the main road at this spot
I went up on the Simookie where some of the Viljoens, including old John himself, were temporarily
established. Old John was out shooting at the time
and I got one of his sons (who afterwards died there,

215

I believe) to go out with me along the river. We
came across any amount of elephant spoor and on
the following day I got hold of them with my
twelve-bore breech-loader, and I never had such a
punishing time in all my life. I was using home-
made cartridges. The bullets I had moulded myself
and made very hard, and the cartridges were filled
almost to the top with fine powder. The recoil was
awful, and it makes my eyes moist even to-day to
think of it. I did not feel it so much at the first two
or three shots, but afterwards each shot brought
excruciating agony. With the first I brought down
a fine bull and satisfied myself that the gun was all
right. During the day I got in several more shots
and secured six cows, my arm growing more painful
with every discharge.

On the following morning I could not lift my
arm. My shoulder and chest were simply black and
blue, very tender and greatly swollen. Suffice it to
say that I could not use my arm for a fortnight and
it did not increase my admiration for the newly-
invented breech-loader, for elephant shooting at any
rate. Owing to the ignorance of the native boys and
my inability to use my arm it took over ten days to
cut and collect the ivory of the elephants I had shot.

About the eleventh or twelfth day we made a
move and got through the Shashi. It was a slow

and painful journey, however, on account of the
outcrop of slate-stone which, hereabouts, stands up
on edge and makes travelling a very rough business.
Before I left the Viljoens the youngster in charge
of the wagons gave me a dog. I hadn't one with
me so the present was very acceptable. That dog,
however, must have come from a coward stock, for
he would never go out at dark. A wolf could come
close up to the wagons and the dog would only lie
still and growl. I tied him outside once or twice,
chained to the carcasses of animals I had shot, but
it was no good; wolves might come close up and feed
at one end of the carcass while the dog would crouch
at the other, growling, but making no attempt to
tackle the thieves.

It was, I think, on the 13th day after shooting the six elephant cows and a bull that I got
through the Shasha from the south side. On the
following morning, at day-break, the dog gave one
or two short barks. I wondered why he should
launch out into anything so ferocious as a little bark
and in the ordinary way would not have bothered,
but it being nearly time to get up, I roused the old
boy and told him to make coffee. After a cup and
a biscuit, I told the boys to inspan and proceed along
the river, and taking a gun—though my shoulder
was still sore—I went out and quickly ascertained

what had caused the placid dog to bark. Not more than 200 yards from the wagons there was the fresh spoor of a very large herd of elephants. After wasting some time while the boy went back to fetch an axe, I followed the spoor, came up with the herd about 2 o'clock in the afternoon and commenced work.

I should here state that since the damage to my shoulder and chest, I had studied that breech-loader and its ways to some advantage and had satisfied myself that I had considerably overloaded the cartridges. It was my first experience with it after big game and I naturally thought I had to put in the largest possible charge of powder in order to carry a bullet through the thick hide of an elephant. Anyway, it was a trifle too much for me, so this time I took out a Westley-Richards fall-block which had practically no recoil whatever.

When I got up alongside a very nice bull I took a shot at him with the small rifle. To me it was like a cap snapping off, after the terrific discharge of the guns I had previously used. I could not believe that it was effective and I felt that if I wanted to shoot elephant I should have to be well supplied with loose cartridges before I would be able to bring my quarry down. I proceeded to empty into my pockets the contents of two big packets of cartridges, while following on the spoor of the big elephant, but judge of my surprise when, just as I got up to him I saw him stagger, put his trunk to the ground and fall.

This was my first experience of a small, but really effective, breech-loader without a bad recoil to it. It delighted me and I quickly profited by it. Driving a number of cows into a bit of open ground, I jumped off my horse and put in seven shots at those with the biggest ivory. Four of the cows quickly came to a standstill and with a couple of additional shots I brought two of these down. Following up the herd I dropped two more. Altogether, I secured one bull and six cows and this in spite of a slow horse which was suffering from a stiff shoulder. It was a revelation to me as to what could be done with a small gun—after my long experience with a huge elephant gun.

I was making my way down towards the river where I expected to see the wagons, when I heard a tremendous rustling among the leaves and then there came into view another huge herd; or it may have been the original herd, turned back by something or other. Unfortunately my old horse was quite used up, and so was I. However I got in one good shot at a fine bull elephant and then followed him up at a jog-trot pace as he was going in the direction of the wagons. He dropped eventually, bringing my total bag for the day to two bulls and six cows.

On the following morning I took my boy on horseback to cut out the ivory. Having picked up the spoor of the first elephant, I said there must be one not far to the back of it, and carefully picking my way, I found the elephant, but not alone. A big lioness was peering over her neck at us!

" Give me the gun! " I shouted to my boy who had been carrying the weapon for me owing to my injured shoulder.

He hurried up and handed it over and then I found I had no cartridges; the boy had them in his pocket! Before he could give me one the lioness had bolted. I quickly followed, knowing there was an opening a short distance ahead, and there I thought I might see her. When I came to the opening, however, all I could see was two dead elephants. I looked all round very closely and carefully and then turning towards the way I came I saw the lioness not far away looking at me! I must have passed quite close to her on making my way to the opening.

Hastily jumping from my horse I fired, but to my amazement missed her. She turned and raced away but, again jumping on my horse, I came

within range of her again and a shot from horseback caught her under the hind leg, injuring the
abdomen. It was not fatal and not really serious
and she could have recovered from it if she had
left it alone, but she sprang into a bush and commenced biting the wound and the bush. I put
another bullet right through her two shoulders, but
this was not sufficient to finish her off for she ran
out to a mopani tree some 200 yards away, where
she paused. I had only one elephant bullet left and
just as I was about to use it I saw my boy coming
along on horseback, right in the line of fire. I
whistled to him, to attract his attention, and with
my hand directed him the way to go.

The idiot went about 50 yards and stood still.
I whistled again and signalled him to get further
away. By this time he was fully 100 yards away
and well out of my line of fire, but not out of danger
from the wounded lioness. I was sitting on my
horse only about 40 yards from the lioness, and
though the boy was twice that distance away, by
some instinct she seemed to know that whilst I was
to be feared, the native was harmless. I put another
bullet right through her, almost in the same hole
as the one I had previously put through her.

With a growl she sprang up and made straight
for the boy. He started jerking his horse's mouth

instead of laying into him with the sjambok. The panic-stricken animal simply threw back its head and refused to move and in one, two, three the lioness had reached the horse, made one leap on to the boy and in a twinkling pulled him off and had him on the ground. There she proceeded to worry him as a terrier worries a rat. At last she stopped and lay still.

I called out to the boy: " Baren."

" Yes, baas," he faintly answered.

" You keep perfectly still now. Don't make the least movement and the lioness will leave you alone, because she will think you are dead."

" Yes, baas," he replied.

I knew I had dropped a cartridge the previous day close to where the two elephants were lying dead in the open and I was in hopes that I might find it now. I went away but had no sooner got on my horse to search for the cartridge, than I heard a scream from the boy. I hastened back and he called out to me that the lioness, which had been lying some five yards off, had pounced upon him again and worried him.

Once more I told him to keep perfectly still, that he had probably brought this second attack upon himself by trying to get away and that if he would only keep still a few minutes longer the lioness would be dead.

I saw her go a little further off. She was staggering and I could see that I had hurt her badly, and that she was on her last legs. Just at this moment I heard a bullock bellow and knowing this would mean that my wagons were near at hand, I again called to the boy to keep perfectly still while I hastened to the wagons to get more cartridges and help.

I galloped in the direction of the sound of the bullock's bellow, and found they had just outspanned. Getting a fresh supply of cartridges, I put another boy on the back of the other horse, which had sustained a nasty wound on the thigh from the lion's hind claws. We galloped as fast as we could to the spot where I had left the boy, but to our amazement he was nowhere to be seen. For a moment I thought the lioness had completely finished him and dragged him away, but she was lying perfectly still on the spot I had last seen her.

" Be ready, John," I said to the boy, " but I think she is dead." We walked slowly forward and, sure enough, she was dead.

Then we followed the spoor of the boy and we could see he had crawled his full length and had then jumped up and ran. I could see by his spoor that he was lame. We overtook him about 200 yards from where the wagons were standing. He had managed to reach a pool of water, where he quenched his thirst and then lay down in the sun. He was in a terrible plight, his many wounds stiff, and he was in a state of collapse. It was a very difficult business getting him on to one of the horses, but at last we carried him to the wagons. Here the boys washed him and dabbed his wounds with carbolic oil, while he told them how he " humbugged " the lioness.

He told, with much detail, how " he had hung his hat and clothes on the stump of a tree to delude her that he was still there, that he had then crawled on his hands and knees for a long distance and when he thought he was out of sight he jumped to his feet and ran for it." A very pretty story, but not borne out by his spoor.

There is no doubt he had had a terrible mauling. The lioness had bitten him on practically every part of his body—ankles, legs, hips, wrists and shoulders —and her teeth had cut a wrist strap through on both sides.

CHAPTER XXIII

TSETSE-FLY AND BUFFALO—MY THEORY—MY FIRST ATTACK
OF FEVER—THE INJURED NATIVE—SAD WAGON ACCI-
DENT—OVERTURNED IN A SWAMP

WE had to stay at this spot for a week in order
to cut out and bring to the wagons the ivory from
the elephants I had shot, several of the animals lying
a considerable distance away. By this time my
shoulder had sufficiently recovered from the punishing effect of the breech-loader that I was able to
help, otherwise we should have been a fortnight or
more over the task.

After loading it all up, we turned our faces to
the south towards the Crocodile River. We got
low down on the river, where I knew there was
" fly " in former days, but on this occasion there was
no sign of fly, neither could we see any buffalo
spoor. As I wished to get a few buffalo, if possible,
I moved to another spot higher up the river where
the buffalo and fly used to be common some years
previously, but here again I was doomed to disappointment—no fly, no buffalo.

The only explanation I can offer is this: When I came out in 1875, "trek-Boers" were simply swarming on the Marico and Crocodile Rivers. In all there must have been some 300 families, and as they were not small families either, and they had practically nothing to live upon but meat, it can readily be imagined the amount of shooting that would be necessary to keep them all going. It was now quite clear that they had shot and driven out the buffalo from those parts and the fly went with them. My own observations on this subject, spread over many years, are that there is a direct association between tsetse-fly and buffalo: that the fly breeds in the buffalo dung and nowhere else, and that when the buffalo is exterminated or driven away, the fly will die out owing to the absence of suitable breeding places. I do not mean to say that it will disappear in one year, but I put three years as the limit. I do not know whether the life history of the tsetse-fly has been thoroughly and completely worked out, but I do not think it has an annual cycle like most flies. So far as I have been able to discover, its history extends over three years, though it is possible that a few may survive the fourth year, but that I should imagine would be the limit.

That buffalo and fly are associated seems to be borne out by the fact that in the Victoria Falls basin there were formerly large herds of buffalo and plenty of fly, and now that there are no buffalo the fly has disappeared. In view of the scare now being raised in connection with sleeping sickness and the possible spread of this disease by means of the common tsetse-fly, *glossina morsitans,* I commend these observations, based on experience, to the authorities and trust that before they commence a campaign, having for its object the ruthless extermination of all the beautiful big game of the Rhodesias and Nyassaland they will establish, beyond all doubt, the present very doubtful theory that the tsetse-fly can exist apart from buffalo. If they find that only buffalo are responsible for the perpetuation of the pest, then it would not take long to wipe them out, and in any event that might be the first step before other species of game are interfered with.

We moved steadily southwards, not making any rapid pace, chiefly out of consideration for the native boy, Baren, who had been so badly bitten and torn by the lion. We had built for him at the back of the buck-wagon a sort of box where he could ride, his injuries being such that he was quite unable to walk or to do anything for himself without assistance. He was very cheerful and used to lie in the box, and exchange lively chatter with the other boys, who were always ready to cheer him up with a joke.

But the sick boy's chief comrade was a Matabele boy about five years old—a lively, amusing little picannin as playful as a kitten. He used to clamber into the box with the sick boy and have a little sleep as the wagon moved along.

It was during the wet season and we made slow progress, for the wagon frequently stuck fast and we sometimes had considerable difficulty in extricating it. One day I had left the wagon and gone ahead on horseback, when one of the boys came running after me to say that the wagon had overturned. I galloped back and found that in trying to get through a swamp, old Hans, who had grown tired of the constant delays, had been a bit impetuous with the oxen, and the result was the huge and heavily laden vehicle had completely overturned, with the injured boy, Baren, and the picannin, underneath.

Baren was still alive, for I heard him call out for help. Telling him we would have him out in a few minutes, I quickly loosened the span of oxen, and with the help of the boys, hooked the span on to the buck to pull it right over. Though we worked as rapidly as possible, some three minutes elapsed before we could move it sufficiently to extricate the boy, pressed down as he was by the weight of all the ivory and enveloped in the buck sail and a quan-

tity of grass he had for a couch. We turned it over
at last, but were just too late. Poor Baren gave his
last gasp just as we released him. The little picannin was quite dead.

We dug two graves and buried them, and it
was a very sad little party that moved away from
this spot, for both Baren and the picannin had been
favourites; their very helplessness made them the
object of everyone's care, and their tragic and unexpected end had a depressing effect.

Some three or four days later I got my first dose
of malaria fever. We had reached the Crocodile
River, not far from where the trek-Boers were
stationed, though they were higher up at the time.

It seems amazing that I should have escaped it
for so many years, but so it was. I do not know to
what my immunity can be attributed. It may have
been owing to the fact that I avoided spirits, it may
have been due to my fine constitution. It may have
been due to the fact that I usually lived well and had
no worry. I cannot say. Lest teetotallers may use
the first of the above suggestions as an argument I
may mention that natives, who do not often get
liquor, get fever. It was certainly not because I
took any precautions against mosquitoes, for the
mosquito theory had not been thought of in those
days and I have slept and hunted in country where

the mosquitoes swarmed to such an extent that one's face would be black with them when one slept. I had my share of mosquito bites, but until now the fever had not reached me.

However, there was no question about it this time and I put it down to the fact that my food was not as good as usual, while I was also harassed and careworn. For fifteen days I lay helpless, racked with the fever. For most of the time I was unconscious and I do not remember what happened, save that I know I craved for long draughts of bitter cold tea, out of the teapot. My boys were in great distress of mind at my condition, but they did their best. They killed two of the oxen to make soup for me, but after they had made it I could not touch it. The bitter tea was all that I wanted.

About the sixteenth day, when I began to get out of the bad stage, three good Samaritans, Capt. Scott, Sandy Anderson and a man named Webster, came upon the scene. Capt. Scott immediately took me in hand and commenced literally to pour gin into me. It was the first time I had ever tasted it in my life and I cannot say it was particularly palatable to me, but the Captain kept giving me copious doses nor would he listen to any of my weak refusals.

"We've got to build you up," was his reply, "and we are going to do it." While he poured the gin into me, his companions laid hands upon a number of ownerless sheep that were about the place—ownerless, because the Matabele had killed or driven away their former native owners. From these sheep these good fellows made me mutton-broth, and for four days gin and mutton-broth alternated every few hours. It effected a most amazing change and soon I was able to get about on horseback and to resume my journey southwards to Kimberley.

My three friends in the wilderness, after receiving my heartfelt thanks for their disinterested kidness and assistance at such a critical time, continued their journey northwards.

It is true that I got a relapse, but not before I was within reach of Kimberley. I went down with the relapse into an even worse condition than I had with the original attack. I collapsed completely and was as near Death's door as any man could safely go and hope to return.

I had been down some ten days, when my brother, who was at Kimberley, heard from some of my friends that if he wanted to see me alive he had better come out at once. He wasted no time, picked me up about eight hours' journey from Kimberley and got me into the town. There I remained in a very bad condition for over three months before I was able to get about again.

CHAPTER XXIV

A FISHING ADVENTURE — WATCHED BY CROCODILES — A
FOREST TRAGEDY—LIONS, ZEBRA AND CROCODILES—
THE SAURIANS' FEAST

I HOPE my readers will forgive me for occasionally going back in my recollections. I have endeavoured to make it a plain, straightforward narrative, but sometimes an incident slips out of one's memory for the moment, to be revived by some chance word. Such a one was an eerie experience I had on my last unlucky trip. It was on my way southward from Lobengula's, before I got the fever. I had reached the Crocodile River, and after outspanning and having a little food to eat, I took a fishing line and hook to the river to try my luck for eel for supper.

I caught two small ones (which, however, subsequently proved remarkably good eating) and would have remained longer, but, call me a coward if you wish, the place was altogether too uncanny for my liking. Every minute or so the big ugly head of a crocodile would appear in the water just in front of me, the owner would give me a long steady stare and then sink out of sight. The place literally swarmed with the brutes, and my nerves soon began to feel the effects of being subjected to such a keen scrutiny by a dozen or more hungry saurians who were anxious to make my acquaintance at their supper table. The people who originally named it the Crocodile River made no mistake! If I had had my heavy gun with me I would have put a few bullets into the crocodiles, but as I had only a shot-gun I could do nothing, and they seemed to know I was powerless to injure them, for in the ordinary way crocodiles keep out of sight when in the water, but these fellows were almost impudent in their keen interest in me. I did not like the spot at all. The reeds and grass were very thick thereabouts, thick enough to shelter all sorts of danger, and I kept a very close watch, not only on the water, but all around me.

Some few yards from where I was sitting I noticed an old rhinoceros footpath leading down to the water. It had been quite well worn by the rhino, but was now apparently used by smaller animals to get to the water. It was a by no means ideal drinking spot for them, for in the first place the bank was very steep, then they had to get down a ledge about a foot in depth and were at once fetlock deep in the water.

I had been sitting near this path altogether for

about an hour when I saw three zebras coming down the path. I kept perfectly still and as I was well concealed I was enabled to watch their movements. They came along very cautiously as though apprehensive of danger, and when about half way down the slope, they stopped and had a look all around them. Apparently satisfied with their scrutiny they continued their progress to the water and scrambled down the ledge.

They had just got their muzzles to the water when suddenly there was a nerve-shaking roar and a huge lion, that had been lying concealed in the reeds, sprang through the air and on to the back of the zebra nearest me.

The impact and the fright caused the three zebras and the lion to fall headlong into the deep water together. With screams of terror two of the zebras managed to scramble out and, hastening up the steep bank, disappeared into the bush.

To my amazement the other one did not reappear above the surface, neither did the lion. For a few seconds the water was agitated as though some terrible tragedy was being enacted beneath, and then there came to the surface eddies of blood, colouring the water all around. I remained for some minutes but the blood gradually disappeared, the surface resumed its former placid appearance and there was nothing to show that another forest tragedy had been enacted. Nothing? Well, the crocodiles had disappeared from view! It would not have taken that hungry, awful mob many seconds to tear both lion and zebra limb from limb.

I stopped fishing after this and hastened back to the wagons without losing any time, this particular neighbourhood being a little too exciting for me. When I got to the wagons the boys were all agog to know what had happened, for they had heard the combined roar of the lion and the screams of the zebras.

When I told them of the fate of the lion, they were clearly startled and promptly voted that we inspan and shift to less dangerous quarters for the night.

CHAPTER XXV

FROM HUNTER TO TRADER—A BIG DEAL—THE BASUTO WAR
—IN "MAJUBA" DAYS—ROBBED BY NATIVES—LIFE IN
JOHANNESBURG—RETURN TO BULAWAYO—SOME FINAL
REFLECTIONS

I AM not sure that the later stages of my career
possess any interest for the general reader, but as
my editor informs me that several people have in-
quired whether I " shuffled off this mortal coil " at
the end of my last hunting trip, it may be as
well to explain that the finish of my hunting days
did not mean the finish of myself. The financial
results of my hunting and trading trips had been
such that I was able to command a fair sum at the
bank, and in the school of experience I had discovered that there was more money and less risk in
trading than in pitting my skill against wild beasts.
Furthermore, my last trip, with the severe attacks
of fever, had engendered in me a feeling—for the
first time in my life—that I was not immune from
the common dangers of the bush veld. Until we get
a serious illness, none of us realise this fact, and
after slipping out of the jaws of death as I had done,
I felt that it was due to myself to leave the strenuous

life to the younger men and to take things quietly.

For two years I remained at Kimberley, gradually rebuilding my shattered constitution, and then, on the opportunity presenting itself, I moved out to Mamusa, not far from the diamond capital, and opened up a trading station there, my customers for the most part being the Koranna natives.

Here I remained for three years and did excellently from a business point of view, trading mealies and Kafir corn against the ordinary articles of barter. During my stay here the Basuto War broke out and the country was scoured for food for the troops. I was the lucky possessor of about 1,200 bags of grain, and though only my own wagons were available for transport, I managed by tremendous efforts to get it into Kimberley where it realised £4 5s. per bag. As it had not cost me more than about 10s. per bag it was worth a struggle to get it into Kimberley at the price above named!

Life jogged along quietly till the Boer War broke out, with the Majuba incident as its termination. I had never been in love with the Boers and made no secret of it, and my exploits with the cannon did not tend to increase their love for me. When, therefore, they came out on top with their country returned to them by the British Government and the Union Jack was hauled down, it was clearly no time for an avowed Britisher to remain within their reach. I never imagined, when I decided to get away for a spell, that things would fall out as they did, so I did nothing more than lock up the store—which was chock-a-block with trading goods worth anything up to £4,000—and leave it in charge of David Mashouw, chief of the Korannas. He was a broken reed and, like most of his kind, a thief by nature, for upon my return some time afterwards I found that that worthy and his people had looted the store of everything it contained. It is no consolation to me to reflect that the Boers, subsequently, practically wiped the Korannas off the face of the earth.

I then moved further into the Transvaal and remained in the rural districts from 1883 to 1887. Then I moved to Johannesburg in the early days of the Witwatersrand boom, and took my little part in the " life " and sport of that amazing community, and though I could many a bright tale unfold I refrain, for mine is a hunter's story and such lively incidents as I could narrate have nothing to do with elephant shooting in the country of the Matabele. The days when men sat down to a game of cards on Friday and did not finish till Monday or Tuesday, when fortunes were won or lost in a night, when a madcap would ride his horse into a store or bar (finding entrance through the window!) and make " hay " of everything, amid the delighted shouts of the sportive bystanders, are among the memories of other days.

Such incidents are probably common to all mining communities where money flows almost like water and the spirit of adventure runs strong in men's veins.

My thoughts, however, were always in the country of my early exploits, and when in the fulness of time the, to me, unexpected thing happened, and the power of the great Matabele chief was broken, I packed my traps and, like many others, moved northwards. To me, of course, it was all familiar country. It was in the year 1894 that I came back to my old hunting grounds, and here I have lived and seen another great immigration of the British race. I had seen Johannesburg rise from a camp to a city, and the process repeated with regard to Bulawayo. That such wonderful changes could be effected in the lifetime of an individual even now fills me with amazement. During my hunting days here the power of the Matabele appeared to be invincible, and I did not expect to see it broken in my time. I had not allowed for the intrepidity of the British—though my own career might have afforded me a slight index to their recklessness and daring—and the ever onward-flowing tide of humanity that overflows from the Old Country.

Maybe others will have, and are having, opportunities of hunting among the big game of the world such as I have attempted to describe in these recollections, though I fancy those days are gone forever. I do not think that any man will ever again see and follow such mighty herds of elephant and big game that once roamed over the spots where towns now stand and the railway pushes its iron way. The great spaces of Africa are being penetrated on all sides, and before the resistless march of the railway and the man with the breech-loader the game inevitably disappears.

Similarly, the aboriginal, if he does not disappear, undergoes a change. Doubtless it is better for civilization that the " indaba " tree should be an object of curiosity to globe-trotters than the place of swift and terrible judgment of a dusky potentate like 'Mzilikatse or Lobengula, and that even incorrigible barbarians should serve their sentences inside the four walls of a comfortable gaol, rather than meet their instant doom in the open air in the presence of the people. Possibly the native appreciates the change; possibly he does not. He may have improved, mentally, morally and spiritually since he took to wearing trousers and learned to read and write, but I have my doubts.

The Matabele, as I knew him in the old days, before he had been spoiled by civilisation, was, take him all in all, a man one could both admire and trust. During all my hunting years I had no reason to regard him as other than a friend. There were occasional lapses from the strict path of honesty, as I have previously mentioned, but these incidents were few and far between, and when the Matabele ruled the land a white man was quite as safe from ill-treatment or theft as he is to-day—perhaps more so! Cruelty, bloodshed and rapine were not the distinguishing traits of the people or their rulers, as some would have us believe.

Well, their day has passed and the day of the big game in Southern Rhodesia is passing, too. In good time I shall also pass to " the happy hunting grounds," but not with regret, for I have lived every hour of a very full life and am just entering upon the three-score-years-and-ten limit. I have been privileged to have adventures and to enjoy such hunting as falls to the lot of few men and come out unscathed; I have seen the face of a continent changed almost out of recognition; yet I am still hale and hearty, able to do a five miles' walk against the boys, to enjoy a companionable pipe and glass and, when the lamps are lit, to draw from memory's store such fragments of a hunter's recollections as have herein been set down.

THE END